PROMISES & PRAYERS

for You in the

MILITARY

from the New International Version

TABLE OF CONTENTS

ARMOR OF GOD

The weapons we fight with are not the weapons of the world. On the contrary, they have divine power to demolish strongholds.

2 CORINTHIANS 10:4

The night is nearly over; the day is almost here. So let us put aside the deeds of darkness and put on the armor of light.

ROMANS 13:12

Since we belong to the day, let us be self-controlled, putting on faith and love as a breastplate, and the hope of salvation as a helmet.

1 THESSALONIANS 5:8

The word of God is living and active.
Sharper than any double-edged sword, it
penetrates even to dividing soul and spirit,
joints and marrow; it judges the thoughts
and attitudes of the heart. Nothing in all
creation is hidden from God's sight.

HEBREWS 4:12–13

As God's chosen people, holy and dearly
loved, clothe yourselves with compassion,
kindness, humility, gentleness and patience.
Bear with each other and forgive whatever
grievances you may have against one
another. Forgive as the Lord forgave you.

COLOSSIANS 3:12–13

The LORD is my strength and my shield;
my heart trusts in him, and I am helped.

PSALM 28:7

You are a shield around me, O LORD;
you bestow glory on me and lift up my head.

PSALM 3:3

I call on you, O God, for you will answer me;
give ear to me and hear my prayer.
Show the wonder of your great love ...
Keep me as the apple of your eye;
hide me in the shadow of your wings
from the wicked who assail me,
from my mortal enemies who surround me.

PSALM 17:6–9

You are my refuge and my shield, O LORD;
I have put my hope in your word.

PSALM 119:114

As for God, his way is perfect;
    the word of the LORD *is flawless.*
He is a shield
    for all who take refuge in him....
It is God who arms me with strength
    and makes my way perfect.

2 SAMUEL 22:31, 33

The LORD *holds victory in store for the upright,*
    he is a shield to those whose walk is
        blameless,
    for he guards the course of the just
    and protects the way of his faithful ones.

PROVERBS 2:7–8

Be strong in the Lord and in his mighty
power. Put on the full armor of God so that
you can take your stand against the devil's
schemes. For our struggle is not against
flesh and blood, but against the rulers,
against the authorities, against the powers of
this dark world and against the spiritual

forces of evil in the heavenly realms. Therefore put on the full armor of God, so that when the day of evil comes, you may be able to stand your ground, and after you have done everything, to stand. Stand firm then, with the belt of truth buckled around your waist, with the breastplate of righteousness in place, and with your feet fitted with the readiness that comes from the gospel of peace. In addition to all this, take up the shield of faith, with which you can extinguish all the flaming arrows of the evil one. Take the helmet of salvation and the sword of the Spirit, which is the word of God. And pray in the Spirit on all occasions with all kinds of prayers and requests. With this in mind, be alert and always keep on praying for all the saints.

EPHESIANS 6:10–18

REFLECTIONS ON TODAY
for Tomorrow

_____

_____

_____

_____

_____

_____

_____

_____

_____

_____

_____

_____

_____

_____

BELIEF

"For God so loved the world that he gave his one and only Son, that whoever believes in him shall not perish but have eternal life."

JOHN 3:16

Jesus said, "I tell you the truth, he who believes has everlasting life."

JOHN 6:47

Without faith it is impossible to please God, because anyone who comes to him must believe that he exists and that he rewards those who earnestly seek him.

HEBREWS 11:6

To all who received him, to those who believed in his name, he gave the right to become children of God.

JOHN 1:12

Then Jesus told him, "Because you have seen me, you have believed; blessed are those who have not seen and yet have believed."

JOHN 20:29

All the prophets testify about him that everyone who believes in him receives forgiveness of sins through his name.

ACTS 10:43

If you confess with your mouth, "Jesus is Lord," and believe in your heart that God raised him from the dead, you will be saved. For it is with your heart that you believe and are justified, and it is with your mouth that you confess and are saved.

ROMANS 10:9–10

Believe in the Lord Jesus, and you will be saved.

ACTS 16:31

Jesus said, "Everything is possible for him who believes."

MARK 9:23

"Whoever believes in the Son has eternal life."

JOHN 3:36

Jesus declared, "I am the bread of life. He who comes to me will never go hungry, and he who believes in me will never be thirsty."

JOHN 6:35

Jesus cried out, "When a man believes in me, he does not believe in me only, but in the one who sent me. When he looks at me, he sees the one who sent me. I have come into the world as a light, so that no one who believes in me should stay in darkness.

JOHN 12:44–46

Everyone who believes that Jesus is the Christ is born of God, and everyone who loves the father loves his child as well. This is how we know that we love the children of God: by loving God and carrying out his commands. This is love for God: to obey his commands. And his commands are not burdensome, for everyone born of God overcomes the world. This is the victory that has overcome the world, even our faith. Who is it that overcomes the world? Only he who believes that Jesus is the Son of God.

1 JOHN 5:1–5

Jesus said, "If you believe, you will receive whatever you ask for in prayer."

MATTHEW 21:22

REFLECTIONS ON TODAY
for Tomorrow

_____

_____

_____

_____

_____

_____

_____

_____

_____

_____

_____

_____

_____

_____

BLESSING

Blessed is the man who trusts in the LORD,
whose confidence is in him.

JEREMIAH 17:7

Praise be to the God and Father of our Lord
Jesus Christ, who has blessed us in the
heavenly realms with every spiritual blessing
in Christ.

EPHESIANS 1:3

How great is your goodness,
which you have stored up for those who
fear you,
which you bestow in the sight of men
on those who take refuge in you.

PSALM 31:19

From the fullness of his grace we have all
received one blessing after another.

JOHN 1:16

There is no difference between Jew and
Gentile—the same Lord is Lord of all and
richly blesses all who call on him, for,
"Everyone who calls on the name of the
Lord will be saved."

ROMANS 10:12–13

Surely, O LORD, you bless the righteous;
you surround them with your favor as
with a shield.

PSALM 5:12

Blessed be your glorious name, and may it be exalted above all blessing and praise. You alone are the LORD. You made the heavens, even the highest heavens, and all their starry host, the earth and all that is on it, the seas and all that is in them. You give life to everything, and the multitudes of heaven worship you.

NEHEMIAH 9:5–6

Give generously to him and do so without a grudging heart; then because of this the LORD your God will bless you in all your work and in everything you put your hand to.

DEUTERONOMY 15:10

May God be gracious to us and bless us
*   and make his face shine upon us,*
that your ways may be known on earth,
*   your salvation among all nations.*
May the peoples praise you, O God;
*   may all the peoples praise you.*
May the nations be glad and sing for joy,
*   for you rule the peoples justly*
*   and guide the nations of the earth.*

PSALM 67:1–4

The LORD gives strength to his people;
*   the LORD blesses his people with peace.*

PSALM 29:11

*Those the L*ORD *blesses will inherit the land.*

PSALM 37:22

Your father's blessings are greater
    than the blessings of the ancient mountains,
    than the bounty of the age-old hills.

GENESIS 49:26

Blessings will come upon you and
accompany you if you obey the LORD
your God.

DEUTERONOMY 28:2

Blessings crown the head of the righteous.

PROVERBS 10:6

REFLECTIONS ON TODAY
for Tomorrow

BOLDNESS

Wait for the LORD;
    be strong and take heart
    and wait for the LORD.

PSALM 27:14

He gives strength to the weary
    and increases the power of the weak.
Even youths grow tired and weary,
    and young men stumble and fall;
but those who hope in the LORD
    will renew their strength.
They will soar on wings like eagles;
    they will run and not grow weary,
    they will walk and not be faint.

ISAIAH 40:29–31

Be strong and courageous. Do not be afraid
or terrified because of them, for the Lord
your God goes with you; he will never leave
you nor forsake you.

DEUTERONOMY 31:6

If God is for us, who can be against us? He
who did not spare his own Son, but gave
him up for us all—how will he not also,
along with him, graciously give us all things?

ROMANS 8:31–32

The Lord is my light and my salvation—
  whom shall I fear?
The Lord is the stronghold of my life—
  of whom shall I be afraid?

PSALM 27:1

Let us hold unswervingly to the hope we profess, for he who promised is faithful.

HEBREWS 10:23

I am not ashamed of the gospel, because it is the power of God for the salvation of everyone who believes.

ROMANS 1:16

I know whom I have believed, and am convinced that he is able to guard what I have entrusted to him for that day.

2 TIMOTHY 1:12

Be strong and courageous. Do not be terrified; do not be discouraged, for the LORD your God will be with you wherever you go.

JOSHUA 1:9

The name of the LORD is a strong tower;
the righteous run to it and are safe.

PROVERBS 18:10

"Let not the wise man boast of his wisdom
or the strong man boast of his strength
or the rich man boast of his riches,
but let him who boasts boast about this:
that he understands and knows me,
that I am the LORD, who exercises kindness,
justice and righteousness on earth,
for in these I delight,"
declares the LORD.

JEREMIAH 9:23–24

Be on your guard; stand firm in the faith; be
men of courage; be strong.

1 CORINTHIANS 16:13

The LORD is my strength and my song;
    he has become my salvation.
He is my God, and I will praise him,
    my father's God, and I will exalt him.

EXODUS 15:2

Love the LORD your God with all your heart
and with all your soul and with all your
strength. These commandments that I give
you today are to be upon your hearts.

DEUTERONOMY 6:5

It is God who arms me with strength
    and makes my way perfect.
He makes my feet like the feet of a deer;
    he enables me to stand on the heights.

2 SAMUEL 22:33–34

REFLECTIONS ON TODAY
for Tomorrow

_____

_____

_____

_____

_____

_____

_____

_____

_____

_____

_____

_____

_____

COMFORT

Praise be to the God and Father of our Lord
Jesus Christ, the Father of compassion and
the God of all comfort, who comforts us in
all our troubles, so that we can comfort
those in any trouble with the comfort we
ourselves have received from God.

2 CORINTHIANS 1:3–4

Jesus said, "In this world you will have
trouble. But take heart! I have overcome
the world."

JOHN 16:33

The LORD is my shepherd, I shall not be in want.
    He makes me lie down in green pastures,
he leads me beside quiet waters,
    he restores my soul.
He guides me in paths of righteousness
    for his name's sake.
Even though I walk
    through the valley of the shadow of death,
I will fear no evil,
    for you are with me;
your rod and your staff,
    they comfort me.

PSALM 23:1–4

Jesus said, "Surely I am with you always, to
the very end of the age."

MATTHEW 28:20

May your unfailing love be my comfort, O LORD,
    according to your promise.

PSALM 119:76

Jesus said, "Peace I leave with you; my peace I give you. I do not give to you as the world gives. Do not let your hearts be troubled and do not be afraid."

JOHN 14:27

Cast all your anxiety on [God] because he cares for you.

1 PETER 5:7

A righteous man may have many troubles,
    but the LORD delivers him from them all.

PSALM 34:19

"I, even I, am he who comforts you,"
    declares the LORD.

ISAIAH 51:12

The LORD is my light and my salvation—
    whom shall I fear?
The LORD is the stronghold of my life—
    of whom shall I be afraid? ...
I am still confident of this:
    I will see the goodness of the LORD
    in the land of the living.
Wait for the LORD;
    be strong and take heart
    and wait for the LORD.

PSALM 27:1, 13–14

The righteous cry out, and the LORD hears them;
    he delivers them from all their troubles.
The LORD is close to the brokenhearted
    and saves those who are crushed in spirit.

PSALM 34:17–18

Through Christ our comfort overflows.

2 CORINTHIANS 1:5

When I said, "My foot is slipping,"
    your love, O LORD, supported me.
When anxiety was great within me,
    your consolation brought joy to my soul.

PSALM 94:18–19

Shout for joy, O heavens;
    rejoice, O earth;
    burst into song, O mountains!
For the LORD comforts his people
    and will have compassion on his
    afflicted ones.

ISAIAH 49:13

REFLECTIONS ON TODAY
for Tomorrow

CONFIDENCE

We say with confidence, "The Lord is my helper; I will not be afraid."

HEBREWS 13:6

is is the confidence we have in
oaching God: that if we ask anything
ding to his will, he hears us. And if we
hat he hears us—whatever we ask—
that we have what we asked

1 JOHN 5:14

righteousness will be peace;
ct of righteousness will be
ess and confidence forever.

ISAIAH 32:17

You have been my hope, O Sovereign LORD,
my confidence since my youth.

PSALM 71:5

The LORD will be your confidence
and will keep your foot from
being snared.

PROVERBS 3:26

Blessed is the man who trusts in the LORD,
whose confidence is in him.

JEREMIAH 17:7

"I have great confidence in you; I take great
pride in you. I am greatly encouraged ...
my joy knows no bounds."

2 CORINTHIANS 7:

Let us then approach the throne of grace with confidence, so that we may receive mercy and find grace to help us in our time of need.

HEBREWS 4:16

Do not throw away your confidence; it will be richly rewarded. You need to persevere so that when you have done the will of God, you will receive what he has promised.

HEBREWS 10:35

Dear friends, if our hearts do not condemn us, we have confidence before God and receive from him anything we ask, because we obey his commands and do what pleases him.

1 JOHN 3:21–22

"I am glad I can have complete confidence in you."

2 CORINTHIANS 7:16

Such confidence as this is ours through Christ before God. Not that we are competent in ourselves to claim anything for ourselves, but our competence comes from God.

2 CORINTHIANS 3:4

Paul said, "In him and through faith in Jesus we may approach God with freedom and confidence. I ask you, therefore, not to be discouraged because of my sufferings for you, which are your glory."

EPHESIANS 3:12–13

We have come to share in Christ if we hold firmly till the end the confidence we had at first.

HEBREWS 3:14

May the Lord direct your hearts into God's love and Christ's perseverance.

2 Thessalonians 3:5

I am still confident of this:
I will see the goodness of the Lord
in the land of the living.

Psalm 27:13

Jesus guided them safely, so they were unafraid.

Psalm 78:53

Jesus said, "Be assured that my words are not false;
one perfect in knowledge is with you."

Job 36:4

REFLECTIONS ON TODAY
for Tomorrow

_____

_____

_____

_____

_____

_____

_____

_____

_____

_____

_____

_____

_____

_____

COURAGE

Be strong and take heart,
*   all you who hope in the LORD.*

PSALM 31:24

The LORD is my strength and my shield;
*   my heart trusts in him, and I am helped.*
My heart leaps for joy
*   and I will give thanks to him in song.*

PSALM 28:7

Be strong and courageous. Do not be
terrified; do not be discouraged, for the
LORD your God will be with you wherever
you go.

JOSHUA 1:9

For God did not give us a spirit of timidity, but a spirit of power, of love and of self-discipline.

2 TIMOTHY 1:7

Be still, and know that I am God.

PSALM 46:10

Jesus said, "Do not be afraid, little flock, for your Father has been pleased to give you the kingdom."

LUKE 12:32

Because the hand of the LORD my God was on me, I took courage.

EZRA 7:28

Blessed is the [one] who fears the LORD, ...
He will have no fear of bad news;
his heart is steadfast, trusting in the LORD.
His heart is secure, he will have no fear.

PSALM 112:7–8

Jesus said, "Do not be afraid. I am the
First and the Last. I am the Living One;
I was dead, and behold I am alive for ever
and ever!"

REVELATION 1:17–18

"I am the LORD, your God,
who takes hold of your right hand
and says to you, Do not fear;
I will help you,"
declares the LORD.

ISAIAH 41:13

For every house is built by someone, but God is the builder of everything. Moses was faithful as a servant in all God's house, testifying to what would be said in the future. But Christ is faithful as a son over God's house. And we are his house, if we hold on to our courage and the hope of which we boast.

HEBREWS 3:4–6

God is our refuge and strength,
*   an ever-present help in trouble.*
Therefore we will not fear, though the earth give way
*   and the mountains fall into the heart of the sea.*

PSALM 46:2

When I called, O LORD, you answered me;
*   you made me bold and stouthearted.*

PSALM 138:3

The God of all grace … will himself
restore you and make you strong,
firm and steadfast.

1 PETER 5:10

The LORD your God is the one who goes
with you to fight for you against your
enemies to give you victory.

DEUTERONOMY 20:4

When I am afraid,
*   I will trust in you.*
In God, whose word I praise,
*   in God I trust; I will not be afraid.*

PSALM 56:3–4

I can do everything through Christ who
gives me strength.

PHILIPPIANS 4:13

REFLECTIONS ON TODAY
for Tomorrow

CREATION

Since the creation of the world God's invisible qualities—his eternal power and divine nature—have been clearly seen, being understood from what has been made, so that men are without excuse.

ROMANS 1:20

Neither height nor depth, nor anything else in all creation, will be able to separate us from the love of God that is in Christ Jesus our LORD.

ROMANS 8:39

If anyone is in Christ, he is a new creation; the old has gone, the new has come!

2 CORINTHIANS 5:17

For he chose us in him before the creation of the world to be holy and blameless in his sight. In love he predestined us to be adopted as his sons through Jesus Christ, in accordance with his pleasure and will—to the praise of his glorious grace, which he has freely given us in the One he loves. In him we have redemption through his blood, the forgiveness of sins, in accordance with the riches of God's grace that he lavished on us with all wisdom and understanding. And he made known to us the mystery of his will according to his good pleasure, which he purposed in Christ, to be put into effect when the times will have reached their fulfillment—to bring all things in heaven and on earth together under one head, even Christ.

EPHESIANS 1:4–10

He is the image of the invisible God, the firstborn over all creation. For by him all things were created: things in heaven and on earth, visible and invisible, whether thrones or powers or rulers or authorities; all things were created by him and for him.

COLOSSIANS 1:15–16

Nothing in all creation is hidden from God's sight. Everything is uncovered and laid bare before the eyes of him to whom we must give account.

HEBREWS 4:13

Jesus was chosen before the creation of the world, but was revealed in these last times for your sake. Through him you believe in God, who raised him from the dead and glorified him, and so your faith and hope are in God.

1 PETER 1:20–21

When the Lord God made the earth and
the heavens—and no shrub of the field had
yet appeared on the earth and no plant of
the field had yet sprung up, for the Lord
God had not sent rain on the earth and
there was no man to work the ground, but
streams came up from the earth and
watered the whole surface of the ground.

GENESIS 2:4–6

*God said, "Be glad and rejoice forever
in what I will create."*

ISAIAH 65:17

God blessed the seventh day and made it
holy, because on it he rested from all the
work of creating that he had done.

GENESIS 2:3

He who forms the mountains,
  creates the wind,
    and reveals his thoughts to man,
he who turns dawn to darkness,
    and treads the high places of the earth—
    the LORD *God Almighty is his name.*

AMOS 4:13

Jesus said, "Father, I want those you have given me to be with me where I am, and to see my glory, the glory you have given me because you loved me before the creation of the world."

JOHN 17:24

In the beginning God created the heavens and the earth.

GENESIS 1:1

REFLECTIONS ON TODAY
for Tomorrow

_____

_____

_____

_____

_____

_____

_____

_____

_____

_____

_____

_____

_____

_____

_____

_____

DEPENDENCE ON GOD

My salvation and my honor depend on God;
* he is my mighty rock, my refuge.*

PSALM 62:7

Will you rely on God for his great strength?
* Will you leave your heavy work to him?*

JOB 39:11

Let him who walks in the dark,
* who has no light,*
trust in the name of the LORD
* and rely on his God.*

ISAIAH 50:10

We know and rely on the love God has for us. God is love. Whoever lives in love lives in God, and God in him.

1 JOHN 4:16

Trust in the LORD with all your heart
*   and lean not on your own understanding;*
in all your ways acknowledge him,
*   and he will make your paths straight.*

PROVERBS 3:5–6

Lean upon the LORD and say,
*   "Is not the LORD among us?*
*   No disaster will come upon us."*

MICAH 3:11

Accept, O LORD, *the willing praise of my mouth,*
and teach me your laws.

PSALM 119:108

Those who know your name will trust in you,
for you, LORD, *have never forsaken those who*
seek you.

PSALM 9:10

I trust in your unfailing love;
my heart rejoices in your salvation.
I will sing to the LORD,
for he has been good to me.

PSALM 13:5–6

God said, "My son, if you accept my words
    and store up my commands within you,
turning your ear to wisdom
    and applying your heart to understanding,
and if you call out for insight
    and cry aloud for understanding,
and if you look for it as for silver
    and search for it as for hidden treasure,
then you will understand the fear of the LORD
    and find the knowledge of God.
For the LORD gives wisdom,
    and from his mouth come knowledge
    and understanding.
He holds victory in store for the upright,
    he is a shield to those whose walk
    is blameless."

PROVERBS 2:1–7

Some trust in chariots and some in horses,
    but we trust in the name of the LORD our God.
They are brought to their knees and fall,
    but we rise up and stand firm.
O LORD, save the king!
    Answer us when we call!

PSALM 20:7–9

In him our hearts rejoice,
    for we trust in his holy name.
May your unfailing love rest upon us, O LORD,
    even as we put our hope in you.

PSALM 33:21–22

REFLECTIONS ON TODAY

for Tomorrow

_____

_____

_____

_____

_____

_____

_____

_____

_____

_____

_____

_____

_____

_____

DEVOTION

If you devote your heart to him
and stretch out your hands to him ...
then you will lift up your face without shame;
you will stand firm and without fear ...
You will be secure, because there is hope;
you will look about you and take your
rest in safety.

JOB 11:13, 15, 18

Guard my life, for I am devoted to you.
You are my God; save your servant
who trusts in you.

PSALM 86:2

Love the LORD your God and keep his
requirements, his decrees, his laws and his
commands always.

DEUTERONOMY 11:1

Love the LORD your God and keep his
requirements, his decrees, his laws and his
commands always.

DEUTERONOMY 11:1

My eyes are fixed on you, O Sovereign LORD;
    in you I take refuge.

PSALM 141:8

Into your hands I commit my spirit;
    redeem me, O LORD, the God of truth.

PSALM 31:5

*Commit your way to the L*ORD*;*
    trust in him and he will do this:
He will make your righteousness shine
    like the dawn, the justice of your cause like the
    noonday sun.
*Be still before the L*ORD *and wait patiently for him;*
    do not fret when men succeed in their ways ...
Refrain from anger and turn from wrath ...
    *those who hope in the L*ORD *will inherit*
    the land.

PSALM 37:5–7, 9

*Commit to the L*ORD *whatever you do,*
    and your plans will succeed.

PROVERBS 16:3

Remember, O LORD, how I have walked
before you faithfully and with wholehearted
devotion and have done what is good in
your eyes.

ISAIAH 38:3

Give thanks to the LORD, *call on his name;*
    make known among the nations what he
    has done.
Sing to him, sing praise to him;
    tell of all his wonderful acts.
Glory in his holy name;
    let the hearts of those who seek the
    Lord rejoice.
Look to the Lord and his strength;
    seek his face always.
Remember the wonders he has done,
    his miracles, and the judgments
    he pronounced.

1 CHRONICLES 16:7–12

The eyes of the LORD range throughout the earth to strengthen those whose hearts are fully committed to him.

2 CHRONICLES 16:9

He who pursues righteousness and love
    finds life, prosperity and honor.

PROVERBS 21:21

God said, "He will call upon me, and I will
answer him;
    I will be with him in trouble,
    I will deliver him and honor him."

PSALM 91:15

My salvation and my honor depend on God;
    he is my mighty rock, my refuge.

PSALM 62:7

"Sacrifice thank offerings to God,
    fulfill your vows to the Most High,
and call upon me in the day of trouble;
    I will deliver you, and you will honor me,"
    says the LORD.

PSALM 50:14–15

REFLECTIONS ON TODAY
for Tomorrow

_____

_____

_____

_____

_____

_____

_____

_____

_____

_____

_____

_____

_____

EMOTIONS

Rejoice in the Lord always. I will say it again: Rejoice! Let your gentleness be evident to all. The Lord is near.

PHILIPPIANS 4:4–5

In my distress I called to the LORD;
  I called out to my God.
From his temple he heard my voice;
  my cry came to his ears.

2 SAMUEL 22:7

To the [one] who pleases him, God gives wisdom, knowledge and happiness.

ECCLESIASTES 2:26

If calamity comes upon us, whether the sword of judgment, or plague or famine, O LORD, we will stand in your presence before this temple that bears your Name and will cry out to you in our distress, and you will hear us and save us.

2 CHRONICLES 20:9

To the LORD I cry aloud,
*   and he answers me from his holy hill.*
I lie down and sleep;
*   I wake again, because the LORD sustains me.*

PSALM 3:4–5

Whatever is true, whatever is noble, whatever is right, whatever is pure, whatever is lovely, whatever is admirable— if anything is excellent or praiseworthy— think about such things.

PHILIPPIANS 4:8

Make my joy complete by being like-minded, having the same love, being one in spirit and purpose. Do nothing out of selfish ambition or vain conceit, but in humility consider others better than yourselves.

PHILIPPIANS 2:2–3

May the righteous be glad
and rejoice before God;
may they be happy and joyful.

PSALM 68:3

A happy heart makes the face cheerful.

PROVERBS 15:13

I will rejoice in the LORD,
I will be joyful in God my Savior.

HABBAKUK 3:18

When times are good, be happy;
    but when times are bad, consider:
God has made the one
    as well as the other.
Therefore, a man cannot discover
    anything about his future.

ECCLESIASTES 7:14

May the righteous be glad
    and rejoice before God;
      may they be happy and joyful.

PSALM 68:3

Be joyful in hope, patient in affliction,
faithful in prayer.

ROMANS 12:12

Worship the LORD with gladness;
*   come before him with joyful songs.*
Know that the LORD is God.
*   It is he who made us, and we are his;*
*   we are his people, the sheep of his pasture.*
Enter his gates with thanksgiving
*   and his courts with praise;*
*   give thanks to him and praise his name.*

PSALM 100:2–4

Be joyful always; pray continually; give
thanks in all circumstances, for this is God's
will for you in Christ Jesus.

1 THESSALONIANS 5:16–18

REFLECTIONS ON TODAY
for Tomorrow

_____

_____

_____

_____

_____

_____

_____

_____

_____

_____

_____

_____

_____

ENCOURAGEMENT

The LORD tends his flock like a shepherd:
    he gathers the lambs in his arms
and carries them close to his heart;
    he gently leads those that have young.

ISAIAH 40:11

May our Lord Jesus Christ himself and God
our Father, who loved us and by his grace
gave us eternal encouragement and good
hope, encourage your hearts and strengthen
you in every good deed and word.

2 THESSALONIANS 2:16–17

You are a shield around me, O LORD;
    you bestow glory on me and lift up my head.

PSALM 68:3

My purpose is that they may be encouraged in heart and united in love, so that they may have the full riches of complete understanding, in order that they may know the mystery of God, namely, Christ, in whom are hidden all the treasures of wisdom and knowledge.

COLOSSIANS 2:2–3

For in the day of trouble
     The LORD will keep me safe in his dwelling;
he will hide me in the shelter of his tabernacle
     and set me high upon a rock.

PSALM 27:5

You hear, O LORD, the desire of the afflicted;
     you encourage them, and you listen to their cry.

PSALM 10:17

I lift up my eyes to the hills—
    where does my help come from?
My help comes from the LORD,
    the Maker of heaven and earth.
He will not let your foot slip—
    he who watches over you will not slumber;
indeed, he who watches over Israel
    will neither slumber nor sleep.
The LORD watches over you—
    the LORD is your shade at your right hand;
the sun will not harm you by day,
    nor the moon by night.
The LORD will keep you from all harm—
    he will watch over your life;
the LORD will watch over your coming and going
    both now and forevermore.

PSALM 121:1–8

Surely God is my help;
    the LORD *is the one who sustains me.*

PSALM 54:4

The God of all grace, who called you to
his eternal glory in Christ, after you have
suffered a little while, will himself restore
you and make you strong, firm and
steadfast.

1 PETER 5:10

"For I know the plans I have for you,"
declares the LORD, "plans to prosper you
and not to harm you, plans to give you hope
and a future."

JEREMIAH 29:11

The Lord your God is with you,
   he is mighty to save.
He will take great delight in you,
   he will quiet you with his love,
   he will rejoice over you with singing.

ZEPHANIAH 3:17

Those who hope in the Lord
   will renew their strength.
They will soar on wings like eagles;
   they will run and not grow weary,
   they will walk and not be faint.

ISAIAH 40:31

REFLECTIONS ON TODAY
for Tomorrow

_____

_____

_____

_____

_____

_____

_____

_____

_____

_____

_____

_____

_____

ETERNAL LIFE

The world and its desires pass away, but the man who does the will of God lives forever.

1 JOHN 2:17

The gift of God is eternal life in Christ Jesus our Lord.

ROMANS 6:23

For God so loved the world that he gave his one and only Son, that whoever believes in him shall not perish but have eternal life.

JOHN 3:16

Now this is eternal life: that they may know you, the only true God, and Jesus Christ, whom you have sent. I have brought you glory on earth by completing the work you gave me to do. And now, Father, glorify me in your presence with the glory I had with you before the world began.

JOHN 17:3–5

Jesus said, "My sheep listen to my voice; I know them, and they follow me. I give them eternal life, and they shall never perish; no one can snatch them out of my hand. My Father, who has given them to me, is greater than all; no one can snatch them out of my Father's hand. I and the Father are one."

JOHN 10:27–30

Having been justified by his grace, we might become heirs having the hope of eternal life.

TITUS 3:7

Jesus said, "I am the resurrection and the life. He who believes in me will live, even though he dies; and whoever lives and believes in me will never die."

JOHN 11:25–26

God has given us eternal life, and this life is in his Son. He who has the Son has life; he who does not have the Son of God does not have life.

1 JOHN 5:11–12

Jesus said, "I tell you the truth, whoever hears my word and believes him who sent me has eternal life."

JOHN 5:24

Jesus said, "My Father's will is that everyone who looks to the Son and believes in him shall have eternal life."

JOHN 6:40

Jesus said, "I know that his command leads to eternal life. So whatever I say is just what the Father has told me to say."

JOHN 12:50

To those who by persistence in doing good seek glory, honor and immortality, God will give eternal life.

ROMANS 2:7

We know also that the Son of God has come and has given us understanding, so that we may know him who is true. And we are in him who is true—even in his Son Jesus Christ. He is the true God and eternal life.

1 JOHN 5:20

I write these things to you who believe in the name of the Son of God so that you may know that you have eternal life. This is the confidence we have in approaching God: that if we ask anything according to his will, he hears us. And if we know that he hears us—whatever we ask—we know that we have what we asked of him.

1 JOHN 5:13–15

Keep yourselves in God's love as you wait for the mercy of our Lord Jesus Christ to bring you to eternal life.

JUDE 1:21

God said, "Everyone who has left houses or brothers or sisters or father or mother or children or fields for my sake will receive a hundred times as much and will inherit eternal life."

MATTHEW 19:29

REFLECTIONS ON TODAY
for Tomorrow

_____

_____

_____

_____

_____

_____

_____

_____

_____

_____

_____

_____

Faith is being sure of what we hope for and
certain of what we do not see.

HEBREWS 11:1

Through him you believe in God, who
raised him from the dead and glorified him,
and so your faith and hope are in God.

1 PETER 1:21

Though you have not seen him, you love
him; and even though you do not see him
now, you believe in him and are filled with
an inexpressible and glorious joy.

1 PETER 1:8

This is a trustworthy saying that deserves full acceptance (and for this we labor and strive), that we have put our hope in the living God, who is the Savior of all men, and especially of those who believe.

1 Timothy 4:9–10

May your unfailing love rest upon us, O Lord,
even as we put our hope in you.

Psalm 33:33

What does the Scripture say? "Abraham believed God, and it was credited to him as righteousness."

Romans 4:3

Since we have been justified through faith, we have peace with God through our Lord Jesus Christ.

Romans 5:1

Jesus said, "I tell you the truth, anyone who has faith in me will do what I have been doing. He will do even greater things than these, because I am going to the Father. And I will do whatever you ask in my name, so that the Son may bring glory to the Father. You may ask me for anything in my name, and I will do it."

JOHN 14:12–14

"I tell you the truth, if you have faith as small as a mustard seed, you can say to this mountain, 'Move from here to there' and it will move. Nothing will be impossible for you," declared Jesus.

MATTHEW 17:20

For the LORD loves the just
*   and will not forsake his faithful ones.*
They will be protected forever.

PSALM 37:28

The prayer offered in faith will make the
sick person well; the Lord will raise him up.
If he has sinned, he will be forgiven.

JAMES 5:15

For the LORD is good and his love endures forever;
his faithfulness continues through all
generations.

PSALM 100:5

The LORD rewards every man for his
righteousness and faithfulness.

1 SAMUEL 26:23

Those who have served well gain an
excellent standing and great assurance in
their faith in Christ Jesus.

1 TIMOTHY 3:13

In Christ and through faith in him we may approach God with freedom and confidence.

EPHESIANS 3:12

You are all sons of God through faith in Christ Jesus, for all of you who were baptized into Christ have clothed yourselves with Christ.

GALATIANS 3:26–27

God redeemed us ...so that by faith we might receive the promise of the Spirit.

GALATIANS 3:14

A faithful man will be richly blessed.

PROVERBS 28:20

REFLECTIONS ON TODAY
for Tomorrow

_____

_____

_____

_____

_____

_____

_____

_____

_____

_____

_____

_____

_____

_____

_____

_____

FAITHFULNESS

The LORD rewards every man for his
righteousness and faithfulness.

ISAIAH 26:23

I do not hide your righteousness in my heart; O LORD,
I speak of your faithfulness and salvation.
I do not conceal your love and your truth
from the great assembly.

PSALM 40:10

For great is your love, reaching to the heavens;
your faithfulness reaches to the skies.
Be exalted, O God, above the heavens;
let your glory be over all the earth.

PSALM 57:10–11

I will praise you with the harp
*   for your faithfulness, O my God;*
I will sing praise to you with the lyre,
*   O Holy One of Israel.*
My lips will shout for joy
*   when I sing praise to you—*
*   I, whom you have redeemed.*

PSALM 71:22–23

You, O LORD, are a compassionate and gracious
God,
*   slow to anger, abounding in love and*
*   faithfulness.*

PSALM 86:15

Love and faithfulness meet together;
righteousness and peace kiss each other.
Faithfulness springs forth from the earth,
and righteousness looks down from heaven.
The LORD will indeed give what is good,
and our land will yield its harvest.
Righteousness goes before him
and prepares the way for his steps.

PSALM 85:10–13

I will sing of the LORD's great love forever;
with my mouth I will make your faithfulness
known through all generations.
I will declare that your love stands firm forever,
that you established your faithfulness in
heaven itself.

PSALM 89:1–2

Let love and faithfulness never leave you;
    bind them around your neck,
        write them on the tablet of your heart.

PROVERBS 3:3

O LORD, you are my God;
    I will exalt you and praise your name,
for in perfect faithfulness
    you have done marvelous things,
        things planned long ago.

ISAIAH 25:1

For the LORD loves the just
    and will not forsake his faithful ones.

PSALM 37:29

The living, the living—they praise you,
    as I am doing today;
fathers tell their children
    about your faithfulness.
The LORD will save me,
    and we will sing with stringed instruments
all the days of our lives
    in the temple of the LORD.

ISAIAH 38:19–20

Know therefore that the LORD your God is God; he is the faithful God, keeping his covenant of love to a thousand generations of those who love him and keep his commands.

DEUTERONOMY 7:9

REFLECTIONS ON TODAY
for Tomorrow

_____

_____

_____

_____

_____

_____

_____

_____

_____

_____

_____

_____

_____

FAMILY

He and all his family were devout and God-fearing; he gave generously to those in need and prayed to God regularly. One day at about three in the afternoon he had a vision. He distinctly saw an angel of God, who came to him and said, "Cornelius!" Cornelius stared at him in fear. "What is it, Lord?" he asked. The angel answered, "Your prayers and gifts to the poor have come up as a memorial offering before God.

ACTS 10:2–4

All the ends of the earth
  will remember and turn to the LORD,
and all the families of the nations
  will bow down before him.

PSALM 22:27

Choose for yourselves this day whom you will serve ... But as for me and my household, we will serve the LORD.

JOSHUA 24:15

For I have chosen him, so that he will direct his children and his household after him to keep the way of the LORD by doing what is right and just, so that the LORD will bring about for Abraham what he has promised him.

GENESIS 18:19

You are ... fellow citizens with God's people and members of God's household.

EPHESIANS 2:19

He decreed statutes for Jacob
  and established the law in Israel,
which he commanded our forefathers
  to teach their children,
so the next generation would know them,
  even the children yet to be born,
  and they in turn would tell their children.
Then they would put their trust in God
  and would not forget his deeds
  but would keep his commands.

PSALM 78:5-7

The husband of but one wife and must
manage his children and his household well.
Those who have served well gain an
excellent standing and great assurance in
their faith in Christ Jesus.

1 TIMOTHY 3:12

How great is the love the Father has lavished on us, that we should be called children of God! And that is what we are!

1 JOHN 3:1

God said, "My people will live in peaceful
    dwelling places,
in secure homes,
    in undisturbed places of rest."

ISAIAH 32:18

Believe in the Lord Jesus, and you will be saved—you and your household.

ACTS 16:31

Just as each of us has one body with many members, and these members do not all have the same function, so in Christ we who are many form one body, and each member belongs to all the others.

ROMANS 12:4–5

The LORD's love is with those who fear him,
and his righteousness with their
children's children.

PSALM 103:17

I was young and now I am old,
yet I have never seen the righteous forsaken
or their children begging bread.
They are always generous and lend freely;
their children will be blessed.

PSALM 37:25–26

REFLECTIONS ON TODAY
for Tomorrow

_____

_____

_____

_____

_____

_____

_____

_____

_____

_____

_____

_____

_____

FORGIVENESS

Be kind and compassionate to one another, forgiving each other, just as in Christ God forgave you.

EPHESIANS 4:32

[God] forgave us all our sins, having canceled the written code, with its regulations, that was against us and that stood opposed to us; he took it away, nailing it to the cross. And having disarmed the powers and authorities, he made a public spectacle of them, triumphing over them by the cross.

COLOSSIANS 2:13–15

Jesus said, "If you forgive men when they sin against you, your heavenly Father will also forgive you."

MATTHEW 6:14

"Forgive, and you will be forgiven."

LUKE 6:37

Paul wrote, "If you forgive anyone, I also forgive him. And what I have forgiven—if there was anything to forgive—I have forgiven in the sight of Christ for your sake."

2 CORINTHIANS 2:10

Jesus said, "When you stand praying, if you hold anything against anyone, forgive him, so that your Father in heaven may forgive you your sins."

MARK 11:25

Peter came to Jesus and asked, "Lord, how many times shall I forgive my brother when he sins against me? Up to seven times?"

Jesus answered, "I tell you, not seven times, but seventy-seven times."

MATTHEW 18:21–22

If we confess our sins, he is faithful and just and will forgive us our sins and purify us from all unrighteousness.

1 JOHN 1:9

"Blessed are the merciful,
   for they will be shown mercy.
Blessed are the pure in heart,
   for they will see God."

MATTHEW 5:7–8

Blessed is he
   whose transgressions are forgiven,
   whose sins are covered.

PSALM 32:1

The LORD is compassionate and gracious,
   slow to anger, abounding in love.
He will not always accuse,
   nor will he harbor his anger forever;
he does not treat us as our sins deserve
   or repay us according to our iniquities.
For as high as the heavens are above the earth,
   so great is his love for those who fear him;
as far as the east is from the west,
   so far has he removed our transgressions from us.
As a father has compassion on his children,
   so the LORD has compassion on those
   who fear him.

                                    PSALM 103:8–13

Have mercy on me, O God,
  according to your unfailing love;
according to your great compassion
  blot out my transgressions.
Wash away all my iniquity
  and cleanse me from my sin.

PSALM 51:1–2

"Come now, let us reason together,"
  says the LORD.
"Though your sins are like scarlet,
  they shall be as white as snow;
though they are red as crimson,
  they shall be like wool."

ISAIAH 1:18

REFLECTIONS ON TODAY
for Tomorrow

_____

_____

_____

_____

_____

_____

_____

_____

_____

_____

_____

_____

_____

_____

FUTURE

Your beginnings will seem humble,
    so prosperous will your future be.

JOB 8:7

Many, O LORD my God,
    are the wonders you have done.
The things you planned for us
    no one can recount to you;
were I to speak and tell of them,
    they would be too many to declare.

PSALM 40:5

"There is hope for your future,"
    declares the LORD.

JEREMIAH 31:17

Know also that wisdom is sweet to your soul;
*   if you find it, there is a future hope for you,*
*   and your hope will not be cut off.*

PROVERBS 24:14

Humble yourselves, therefore, under God's mighty hand, that he may lift you up in due time.

1 PETER 5:6

Posterity will serve him;
*   future generations will be told about the LORD.*
They will proclaim his righteousness
*   to a people yet unborn.*

PSALM 22:30–31

Jesus said, "I say to all of you: In the future you will see the Son of Man sitting at the right hand of the Mighty One and coming on the clouds of heaven."

MATTHEW 26:64

I am convinced that neither death nor life, neither angels nor demons, neither the present nor the future, nor any powers, neither height nor depth, nor anything else in all creation, will be able to separate us from the love of God that is in Christ Jesus our Lord.

ROMANS 8:38–39

Jesus said, "Do not worry about tomorrow, for tomorrow will worry about itself."

MATTHEW 6:34

Dear friends, now we are children of God, and what we will be has not yet been made known. But we know that when he appears, we shall be like him, for we shall see him as he is. Everyone who has this hope in him purifies himself, just as he is pure.

1 JOHN 3:2-3

The plans of the LORD stand firm forever,
the purposes of his heart through all
generations.

PSALM 33:11

Consider the blameless, observe the upright;
there is a future for the man of peace.

PSALM 37:37

No eye has seen,
    no ear has heard,
no mind has conceived what God has
    prepared for those who love him—

but God has revealed it to us by his Spirit.
The Spirit searches all things, even the deep
things of God.

1 CORINTHIANS 2:9–10

All the days ordained for me
    were written in your book
    before one of them came to be.

PSALM 139:16

"I make known the end from the beginning,
    from ancient times, what is still to come,"
    says the LORD.

ISAIAH 46:10

REFLECTIONS ON TODAY
for Tomorrow

_____

_____

_____

_____

_____

_____

_____

_____

_____

_____

_____

_____

_____

_____

_____

GOD'S LOVE

Jesus said, "Whoever has my commands and obeys them, he is the one who loves me. He who loves me will be loved by my Father, and I too will love him and show myself to him."

JOHN 14:21

The LORD will show compassion,
so great is his unfailing love.

LAMENTATIONS 3:32

We know and rely on the love God has for us. God is love.

1 JOHN 4:16

Jesus said, "If anyone loves me, he will obey my teaching. My Father will love him, and we will come to him and make our home with him."

JOHN 14:23

The LORD *appeared to us in the past, saying:*
"I have loved you with an everlasting love;
*   I have drawn you with loving-kindness."*

JEREMIAH 31:3

This is how we know what love is: Jesus Christ laid down his life for us.

1 JOHN 3:16

The LORD your God loves you.

DEUTERONOMY 23:5

May your unfailing love rest upon us, O LORD,
even as we put our hope in you.

It was just before the Passover Feast. Jesus knew that the time had come for him to leave this world and go to the Father. Having loved his own who were in the world, he now showed them the full extent of his love.

JOHN 13:1

Your love, O LORD, reaches to the heavens,
your faithfulness to the skies.

PSALM 36:5

The LORD *loves righteousness and justice;*
the earth is full of his unfailing love.
By the word of the LORD *were the heavens made,*
their starry host by the breath of his mouth.
He gathers the waters of the sea into jars;
he puts the deep into storehouses.
Let all the earth fear the LORD;
let all the people of the world revere him.

PSALM 33:5–8

The LORD *disciplines those he loves,*
as a father the son he delights in.

PROVERBS 3:12

I trust in your unfailing love, O LORD;
my heart rejoices in your salvation.

PSALM 13:5

You are a forgiving God, gracious and compassionate, slow to anger and abounding in love.

NEHEMIAH 9:17

*"Though the mountains be shaken
and the hills be removed,
yet my unfailing love for you will not be shaken
nor my covenant of peace be removed,"
says the* LORD, *who has compassion on you.*

ISAIAH 54:10

May the grace of the Lord Jesus Christ, and the love of God, and the fellowship of the Holy Spirit be with you all.

2 CORINTHIANS 13:14

REFLECTIONS ON TODAY
for Tomorrow

_____

_____

_____

_____

_____

_____

_____

_____

_____

_____

_____

_____

_____

_____

_____

GOODNESS OF GOD

The LORD is good to all;
*   he has compassion on all he has made.*

PSALM 145:9

Good and upright is the LORD;
*   therefore he instructs sinners in his ways.*
He guides the humble in what is right
*   and teaches them his way.*
All the ways of the LORD are loving and faithful
*   for those who keep the demands of his*
*   covenant.*

PSALM 25:8–10

Answer me, O LORD, out of the goodness of your love;
*   in your great mercy turn to me.*

PSALM 69:16

*The L*ORD *is good,*
   a refuge in times of trouble.
He cares for those who trust in him.

NAHUM 1:7

*How great is your goodness, O L*ORD*,*
   which you have stored up for those who fear
   you,
which you bestow in the sight of men
   on those who take refuge in you.

PSALM 31:19

His divine power has given us everything we
need for life and godliness through our
knowledge of him who called us by his own
glory and goodness.

2 PETER 1:3

The LORD is good to those whose hope is in him,
    to the one who seeks him;
it is good to wait quietly
    for the salvation of the LORD.

LAMENTATIONS 3:25–26

Praise the LORD, for the LORD is good;
    sing praise to his name, for that is pleasant.

PSALM 135:3

Jesus said, "I am the good shepherd;
I know my sheep and my sheep know me—
just as the Father knows me and I know the
Father—and I lay down my life for
the sheep."

JOHN 10:14

The LORD said, "I will cause all my goodness
to pass in front of you, and I will proclaim
my name, the LORD, in your presence. I will
have mercy on whom I will have mercy, and
I will have compassion on whom I will have
compassion."

EXODUS 33:19

We know that in all things God works for
the good of those who love him, who have
been called according to his purpose.

ROMANS 8:28

He is the LORD; let him do what is good
in his eyes.

1 SAMUEL 3:18

Give thanks to the LORD, for he is good;
his love endures forever.

1 CHRONICLES 16:34

You are forgiving and good, O LORD,
abounding in love to all who call to you.
Hear my prayer, O LORD;
listen to my cry for mercy.
In the day of my trouble I will call to you,
for you will answer me.

PSALM 86:5–7

For the LORD God is a sun and shield;
the LORD bestows favor and honor;
no good thing does he withhold
from those whose walk is blameless.

PSALM 84:11

REFLECTIONS ON TODAY
for Tomorrow

GRACE

God is able to make all grace abound to you, so that in all things at all times, having all that you need, you will abound in every good work.

2 CORINTHIANS 9:8

God raised us up with Christ and seated us with him in the heavenly realms in Christ Jesus, in order that in the coming ages he might show the incomparable riches of his grace, expressed in his kindness to us in Christ Jesus.

EPHESIANS 2:6–7

Grace and peace from God the Father and Christ Jesus our Savior.

TITUS 1:4

For you know the grace of our Lord Jesus
Christ, that though he was rich, yet for your
sakes he became poor, so that you through
his poverty might become rich.

2 CORINTHIANS 8:9

The LORD is gracious and righteous;
our God is full of compassion.

PSALM 116:5

Grace and peace be yours in abundance
through the knowledge of God and of Jesus
our Lord.

2 PETER 1:2

God saved us, not because of righteous things we had done, but because of his mercy. He saved us through the washing of rebirth and renewal by the Holy Spirit, whom he poured out on us generously through Jesus Christ our Savior.

TITUS 3:5–6

Grace, mercy and peace from God the Father and from Jesus Christ, the Father's Son, will be with us in truth and love.

2 JOHN 1:3

To each one of us grace has been given as Christ apportioned it.

EPHESIANS 4:7

Righteousness from God comes through faith in Jesus Christ to all who believe. There is no difference, for all have sinned and fall short of the glory of God, and are justified freely by his grace through the redemption that came by Christ Jesus.

ROMANS 3:22–24

I commit you to God and to the word of his grace, which can build you up and give you an inheritance among all those who are sanctified.

ACTS 20:32

By the grace of God I am what I am, and his grace to me was not without effect.

1 CORINTHIANS 15:10

The Word became flesh and made his dwelling among us. We have seen his glory, the glory of the One and Only, who came from the Father, full of grace and truth.

JOHN 1:14

The gracious hand of our God is on everyone who looks to him.

EZRA 8:22

May God be gracious to us and bless us
and make his face shine upon us.

PSALM 67:1

We believe that it is through the grace of our Lord Jesus that we are saved.

ACTS 15:11

REFLECTIONS ON TODAY
for Tomorrow

_____

_____

_____

_____

_____

_____

_____

_____

_____

_____

_____

_____

GUIDANCE

"I will instruct you and teach you in the way you
should go;
I will counsel you and watch over you,"
says the LORD.

PSALM 32:8

Whether you turn to the right or to the left,
your ears will hear a voice behind you,
saying, "This is the way; walk in it."

ISAIAH 30:21

Plans fail for lack of counsel,
but with many advisers they succeed.

PROVERBS 15:22

You guide me with your counsel, O LORD,
   and afterward you will take me into glory.

PSALM 73:24

Your word is a lamp to my feet,
   and a light for my path.

PSALM 119:105

I guide you in the way of wisdom
   and lead you along straight paths.
When you walk, your steps will not be hampered;
   when you run, you will not stumble.
Hold on to instruction, do not let it go;
   guard it well, for it is your life.

PROVERBS 4:11–13

You are my rock and my fortress, O LORD,
   for the sake of your name lead and guide me.

PSALM 31:3

The LORD *will guide you always;*
    he will satisfy your needs in a
    sun-scorched land
    and will strengthen your frame.
You will be like a well-watered garden,
    like a spring whose waters never fail.

ISAIAH 58:11

Show me your ways, O LORD,
    teach me your paths.

PSALM 25:4

Thanks be to God, who always leads us in
triumphal procession in Christ and through
us spreads everywhere the fragrance of the
knowledge of him.

2 CORINTHIANS 2:14

Send forth your light and your truth, O God,
*   let them guide me, O God;*
let them bring me to your holy mountain,
*   to the place where you dwell.*

PSALM 43:3

A wise man's heart guides his mouth,
*   and his lips promote instruction.*
Pleasant words are a honeycomb,
*   sweet to the soul and healing to the bones.*

PROVERBS 16:23–24

"I will give you shepherds after my own heart, who will lead you with knowledge and understanding," says the LORD.

JEREMIAH 3:15

He stilled the storm to a whisper;
     the waves of the sea were hushed.
They were glad when it grew calm,
     and he guided them to their desired haven.
Let them give thanks to the LORD for his
     unfailing love
     and his wonderful deeds for men.

PSALM 107:29–31

Jesus said, "When he, the Spirit of truth, comes, he will guide you into all truth. He will not speak on his own; he will speak only what he hears, and he will tell you what is yet to come."

JOHN 16:13

For this God is our God for ever and ever;
     he will be our guide even to the end.

PSALM 48:14

REFLECTIONS ON TODAY
for Tomorrow

_____

_____

_____

_____

_____

_____

_____

_____

_____

_____

_____

_____

_____

HEAVEN

Jesus said, "In my Father's house are many rooms; if it were not so, I would have told you. I am going there to prepare a place for you. And if I go and prepare a place for you, I will come back and take you to be with me that you also may be where I am. You know the way to the place where I am going."

JOHN 14:2–4

Our citizenship is in heaven. And we eagerly await a Savior from there, the Lord Jesus Christ.

PHILIPPIANS 3:20

Jesus said, "Rejoice that your names are written in heaven."

LUKE 10:20

In keeping with God's promise we are looking forward to a new heaven and a new earth, the home of righteousness.

2 PETER 3:13

Never again will they hunger;
*   never again will they thirst.*
The sun will not beat upon them,
*   nor any scorching heat.*
For the Lamb at the center of the throne
*   will be their shepherd;*
*   he will lead them to springs of living water.*
*   And God will wipe away every tear*
*   from their eyes.*

REVELATION 7:16–17

Acknowledge and take to heart this day that the LORD is God in heaven above and on the earth below. There is no other.

DEUTERONOMY 4:39

Nothing impure will ever enter [heaven], nor will anyone who does what is shameful or deceitful, but only those whose names are written in the Lamb's book of life.

REVELATION 21:27

Now we know that if the earthly tent we live in is destroyed, we have a building from God, an eternal house in heaven, not built by human hands.

2 CORINTHIANS 5:1

[The angel] carried me away in the Spirit to a mountain great and high, and showed me the Holy City, Jerusalem, coming down out of heaven from God. It shone with the glory of God, and its brilliance was like that of a very precious jewel, like a jasper, clear as crystal.

REVELATION 21:10–11

Our citizenship is in heaven. And we eagerly await a Savior from there, the Lord Jesus Christ, who, by the power that enables him to bring everything under his control, will transform our lowly bodies so that they will be like his glorious body.

PHILIPPIANS 3:20

According to the Lord's own word, we tell you that we who are still alive, who are left till the coming of the Lord, will certainly not precede those who have fallen asleep. For the Lord himself will come down from heaven, with a loud command, with the voice of the archangel and with the trumpet call of God, and the dead in Christ will rise first. After that, we who are still alive and are left will be caught up together with them in the clouds to meet the Lord in the air. And so we will be with the Lord forever.

1 THESSALONIANS 4:15–17

Blessed are those who wash their robes, that they may have the right to the tree of life and may go through the gates into the city.

REVELATION 22:14

Yours, O LORD, is the greatness and the power
    and the glory and the majesty and
    the splendor,
    for everything in heaven and earth is yours.
Yours, O LORD, is the kingdom;
    you are exalted as head over all.

1 CHRONICLES 29:11

You alone are the LORD. You made the heavens, even the highest heavens, and all their starry host, the earth and all that is on it, the seas and all that is in them. You give life to everything, and the multitudes of heaven worship you.

NEHEMIAH 9:6

REFLECTIONS ON TODAY
for Tomorrow

_____

_____

_____

_____

_____

_____

_____

_____

_____

_____

_____

_____

_____

HONESTY

Surely you desire truth in the inner parts;
you teach me wisdom in the inmost place.

PSALM 51:6

Honest scales and balances are from the LORD;
all the weights in the bag are of his making.

PROVERBS 16:11

Dear children, let us not love with words or
tongue but with actions and in truth. This
then is how we know that we belong to the
truth, and how we set our hearts at rest in
his presence whenever our hearts condemn
us. For God is greater than our hearts, and
he knows everything.

1 JOHN 3:18–20

He who walks righteously
    and speaks what is right ...
this is the man who will dwell on the heights,
    whose refuge will be the mountain fortress.
His bread will be supplied,
    and water will not fail him.

ISAIAH 33:15–16

Kings take pleasure in honest lips;
    they value a man who speaks the truth.

PROVERBS 16:13

An honest answer
    is like a kiss on the lips.

PROVERBS 24:26

Your love is ever before me,
*   and I walk continually in your truth.*
I do not sit with deceitful men,
*   nor do I consort with hypocrites.*
I wash my hands in innocence,
*   and go about your altar, O LORD,*
proclaiming aloud your praise
*   and telling of all your wonderful deeds....*
I lead a blameless life;
*   redeem me and be merciful to me.*
My feet stand on level ground;
*   in the great assembly I will praise the LORD.*

PSALM 26:3–4, 6–7, 11–12

"I, the LORD, speak the truth;
*   I declare what is right."*

ISAIAH 45:19

I do not hide your righteousness in my heart;
*   I speak of your faithfulness and salvation.*
I do not conceal your love and your truth
*   from the great assembly.*
Do not withhold your mercy from me, O LORD;
*   may your love and your truth always*
*   protect me.*

PSALM 40:10–11

Jesus said, "Whoever can be trusted with
very little can also be trusted with much,
and whoever is dishonest with very little
will also be dishonest with much."

LUKE 16:10

Select capable men from all the people—
men who fear God, trustworthy men who
hate dishonest gain—and appoint them
as officials over thousands, hundreds,
fifties and tens.

EXODUS 18:21

Do not pervert justice or show partiality. Do not accept a bribe, for a bribe blinds the eyes of the wise and twists the words of the righteous. Follow justice and justice alone, so that you may live and possess the land the LORD your God is giving you.

DEUTERONOMY 16:19–20

He whose walk is blameless
    and who does what is righteous,
who speaks the truth from his heart ...
He who does these things
    will never be shaken.

PSALM 15:2, 5

An honest answer
    is like a kiss on the lips.

PROVERBS 24:26

REFLECTIONS ON TODAY
for Tomorrow

_____

_____

_____

_____

_____

_____

_____

_____

_____

_____

_____

_____

_____

_____

HOPE

This I call to mind,
*   and therefore I have hope:*
*Because of the L*ORD*'s great love we are*
*   not consumed,*
*   for his compassions never fail.*

LAMENTATIONS 3:21–22

Praise be to the God and Father of our Lord Jesus Christ! In his great mercy he has given us new birth into a living hope through the resurrection of Jesus Christ from the dead.

1 PETER 1:3

*We wait in hope for the L*ORD*;*
*   he is our help and our shield.*

PSALM 33:20

The LORD delights in those who fear him,
who put their hope in his unfailing love.

PSALM 147:11

Hope does not disappoint us, because God
has poured out his love into our hearts by
the Holy Spirit, whom he has given us.

ROMANS 5:5

"I am the LORD;
those who hope in me will not
be disappointed."

ISAIAH 49:23

Sustain me according to your promise,
*   and I will live;*
*   do not let my hopes be dashed.*
Uphold me, and I will be delivered;
*   I will always have regard for your decrees.*

PSALM 119:116–117

Find rest, O my soul, in God alone;
*   my hope comes from him.*

PSALM 62:5

Everything that was written in the past was
written to teach us, so that through
endurance and the encouragement of the
Scriptures we might have hope.

ROMANS 15:4

Hope that is seen is no hope at all. Who hopes for what he already has? But if we hope for what we do not yet have, we wait for it patiently.

ROMANS 8:24–25

You know with all your heart and soul that not one of all the good promises the LORD your God gave you has failed. Every promise has been fulfilled; not one has failed.

JOSHUA 23:14

Those who hope in the LORD will
inherit the land.

PSALM 37:9

We rejoice in the hope of the glory of God. Not only so, but we also rejoice in our sufferings, because we know that suffering produces perseverance; perseverance, character; and character, hope. And hope does not disappoint us, because God has poured out his love into our hearts by the Holy Spirit, whom he has given us.

ROMANS 5:2–5

The eyes of the LORD are on those who fear him, on those whose hope is in his unfailing love.

PSALM 33:18

May the God of hope fill you with all joy and peace as you trust in him, so that you may overflow with hope by the power of the Holy Spirit.

ROMANS 15:13

REFLECTIONS ON TODAY
for Tomorrow

_____

_____

_____

_____

_____

_____

_____

_____

_____

_____

_____

_____

_____

IDENTITY

The LORD God formed the man from the dust of the ground and breathed into his nostrils the breath of life, and the man became a living being.

GENESIS 2:7

When God created man, he made him in the likeness of God. He created them male and female and blessed them.

GENESIS 5:1–2

We are God's workmanship, created in Christ Jesus to do good works, which God prepared in advance for us to do.

EPHESIANS 2:10

For you created my inmost being, O Lord,
*   you knit me together in my mother's womb.*
I praise you because I am fearfully and
*   wonderfully made;*
*   your works are wonderful,*
*   I know that full well.*
My frame was not hidden from you
*   when I was made in the secret place.*
When I was woven together in the depths
*   of the earth,*
*   your eyes saw my unformed body.*
All the days ordained for me
*   were written in your book*
*   before one of them came to be.*

PSALM 139:13–16

You are all sons of the light and sons
of the day.

1 THESSALONIANS 5:5

What is man that you are mindful of him,
  the son of man that you care for him?
You made him a little lower than the
    heavenly beings
    and crowned him with glory and honor.
You made him ruler over the works of your hands;
  you put everything under his feet:
all flocks and herds,
  and the beasts of the field,
the birds of the air,
  and the fish of the sea,
  all that swim the paths of the seas.
O LORD, our LORD,
  how majestic is your name in all the earth!

PSALM 8:4–9

You were like sheep going astray, but now
you have returned to the Shepherd and
Overseer of your souls.

1 PETER 2:25

Those who are led by the Spirit of God are sons of God. For you did not receive a spirit that makes you a slave again to fear, but you received the Spirit of sonship. And by him we cry, "*Abba*, Father." The Spirit himself testifies with our spirit that we are God's children.

ROMANS 8:14–16

From one man God made every nation of men, that they should inhabit the whole earth; and he determined the times set for them and the exact places where they should live. ... 'For in God we live and move and have our being.' ...
'We are his offspring.'

ACTS 17:26, 28

You yourselves are God's temple and... God's Spirit lives in you.

1 CORINTHIANS 3:16

You are no longer foreigners and aliens, but fellow citizens with God's people and members of God's household, built on the foundation of the apostles and prophets, with Christ Jesus himself as the chief cornerstone. In him the whole building is joined together and rises to become a holy temple in the Lord. And in him you too are being built together to become a dwelling in which God lives by his Spirit.

Ephesians 2:19–22

You are a chosen people, a royal priesthood, a holy nation, a people belonging to God, that you may declare the praises of him who called you out of darkness into his wonderful light.

1 Peter 2:9

Reflections On Today
for Tomorrow

_____

_____

_____

_____

_____

_____

_____

_____

_____

_____

_____

_____

_____

INTEGRITY

The righteous man leads a blameless life;
blessed are his children after him.

PROVERBS 20:7

"I the LORD search the heart
and examine the mind,
to reward a man according to his conduct,
according to what his deeds deserve."

JEREMIAH 17:10

May integrity and uprightness protect me,
because my hope is in you, O God.

PSALM 25:21

LORD, who may dwell in your sanctuary?
  Who may live on your holy hill?
He whose walk is blameless
  and who does what is righteous,
who speaks the truth from his heart
  and has no slander on his tongue,
who does his neighbor no wrong
  and casts no slur on his fellowman,
who despises a vile man
  but honors those who fear the LORD,
who keeps his oath
  even when it hurts,
who lends his money without usury
  and does not accept a bribe against
  the innocent.
He who does these things
  will never be shaken.

PSALM 15:1–5

*For the L*ORD *is righteous,*
   he loves justice;
   upright men will see his face.

PSALM 11:7

In everything set them an example by doing
what is good. In your teaching show integrity,
seriousness and soundness of speech that
cannot be condemned, so that those who
oppose you may be ashamed because they
have nothing bad to say about us. TITUS 2:7–8

The man of integrity walks securely.

PROVERBS 10:9

Who, then, is the man that fears the LORD?
   He will instruct him in the way chosen
   for him.
He will spend his days in prosperity,
   and his descendants will inherit the land.
The LORD confides in those who fear him;
   he makes his covenant known to them.

PSALM 25:12–14

The days of the blameless are known to the LORD,
   and their inheritance will endure forever.

PSALM 37:18

The prayer of a righteous man is powerful
and effective.

JAMES 5:16

Blessed is the man
*   who does not walk in the counsel of the wicked*
or stand in the way of sinners
*   or sit in the seat of mockers.*
*But his delight is in the law of the L*ORD*,*
*   and on his law he meditates day and night.*
He is like a tree planted by streams of water,
*   which yields its fruit in season*
and whose leaf does not wither.
*   Whatever he does prospers.*

PSALM 1:1–3

I know, my God, that you test the heart and
are pleased with integrity.

1 CHRONICLES 29:17

REFLECTIONS ON TODAY
for Tomorrow

_____

_____

_____

_____

_____

_____

_____

_____

_____

_____

_____

_____

JOY

Though you have not seen him, you love
him; and even though you do not see him
now, you believe in him and are filled with
an inexpressible and glorious joy, for you are
receiving the goal of your faith, the salvation
of your souls.

1 PETER 1:8–9

Jesus said, "As the Father has loved me, so
have I loved you. Now remain in my love. If
you obey my commands, you will remain in
my love, just as I have obeyed my Father's
commands and remain in his love. I have
told you this so that my joy may be in you
and that your joy may be complete."

JOHN 15:9–11

The joy of the LORD is your strength.

NEHEMIAH 8:10

You will go out in joy
*   and be led forth in peace;*
the mountains and hills
*   will burst into song before you,*
and all the trees of the field
*   will clap their hands.*

ISAIAH 55:12

A cheerful look brings joy to the heart,
*   and good news gives health to the bones.*

PROVERBS 15:30

God will yet fill your mouth with laughter
*   and your lips with shouts of joy.*

JOB 8:21

Our mouths were filled with laughter,
*   our tongues with songs of joy.*
Then it was said among the nations,
*   "The LORD has done great things for them."*

PSALM 126:2

Jesus said, "Ask and you will receive, and
your joy will be complete."

JOHN 16:24

A highway will be there;
*   it will be called the Way of Holiness. . . .*
Only the redeemed will walk there,
*   and the ransomed of the LORD will return.*
They will enter Zion with singing;
*   everlasting joy will crown their heads.*
Gladness and joy will overtake them,
*   and sorrow and sighing will flee away.*

ISAIAH 35:8–10

You turned my wailing into dancing;
  you removed my sackcloth and clothed
  me with joy,
that my heart may sing to you and not be silent.
  O LORD my God, I will give you
  thanks forever.

PSALM 30:11–12

You have made known to me the path of life,
you will fill me with joy in your presence,
  with eternal pleasures at your right hand.

PSALM 16:11

The prospect of the righteous is joy.

PROVERBS 10:28

In the presence of the LORD your God, you
and your families shall eat and shall rejoice in
everything you have put your hand to,
because the LORD your God has blessed you.

DEUTERONOMY 12:7

Light is shed upon the righteous
  and joy on the upright in heart.
Rejoice in the LORD, you who are righteous,
  and praise his holy name.

PSALM 97:11–12

When anxiety was great within me,
  your consolation brought joy to my soul,
  O LORD.

PSALM 94:19

REFLECTIONS ON TODAY
for Tomorrow

_____

_____

_____

_____

_____

_____

_____

_____

_____

_____

_____

_____

_____

_____

_____

JUSTICE

He has showed you, O man, what is good.
   And what does the LORD require of you?
To act justly and to love mercy
   and to walk humbly with your God.

MICAH 6:8

For it is not those who hear the law who are righteous in God's sight, but it is those who obey the law who will be declared righteous.

ROMANS 2:13

The LORD works righteousness
   and justice for all the oppressed.

PSALM 103:6

This is what the LORD Almighty says: "Administer true justice; show mercy and compassion to one another."

ZECHARIAH 7:9

> *Learn to do right!*
> *Seek justice,*
> *encourage the oppressed.*
> *Defend the cause of the fatherless,*
> *plead the case of the widow.*

ISAIAH 1:17

Do not pervert justice; do not show partiality to the poor or favoritism to the great, but judge your neighbor fairly.

LEVITICUS 19:15

Speak up for those who cannot speak
    for themselves,
    for the rights of all who are destitute.
Speak up and judge fairly;
    defend the rights of the poor and needy.

PROVERBS 31:8–9

The LORD longs to be gracious to you;
    he rises to show you compassion.
For the LORD is a God of justice.
    Blessed are all who wait for him!

ISAIAH 30:18

He is the Rock, his works are perfect,
    and all his ways are just.

DEUTERONOMY 32:4

*The works of the LORD's hands are faithful
    and just;
    all his precepts are trustworthy.
They are steadfast for ever and ever,
    done in faithfulness and uprightness.
He provided redemption for his people;
    he ordained his covenant forever—
    holy and awesome is his name.*

PSALM 111:7–9

For true and just are God's judgments.

REVELATION 19:2

Follow justice and justice alone, so that you
may live and possess the land the LORD your
God is giving you.

DEUTERONOMY 16:20

May the nations be glad and sing for joy,
*   for you rule the peoples justly*
*   and guide the nations of the earth, O Lord.*

PSALM 67:4

God's judgment is right, and as a result
you will be counted worthy of the
kingdom of God.

2 THESSALONIANS 1:5

The Lord is slow to anger and great in power;
*   the Lord will not leave the guilty*
*   unpunished.*
His way is in the whirlwind and the storm,
*   and clouds are the dust of his feet.*

NAHUM 1:3

REFLECTIONS ON TODAY
for Tomorrow

_____

_____

_____

_____

_____

_____

_____

_____

_____

_____

_____

_____

_____

_____

LEADERSHIP

We have different gifts, according to the grace given us. If a man's gift is prophesying, let him use it in proportion to his faith. If it is serving, let him serve; if it is teaching, let him teach; if it is encouraging, let him encourage; if it is contributing to the needs of others, let him give generously; if it is leadership, let him govern diligently.

ROMANS 12:6–8

LORD God, give me wisdom and knowledge, that I may lead.

2 CHRONICLES 1:10

"When one rules over men in righteousness,
when he rules in the fear of God,
he is like the light of morning at sunrise
on a cloudless morning,
like the brightness after rain
that brings the grass from the earth."

2 SAMUEL 23:3-4

Be shepherds of God's flock that is under your care, serving as overseers—not because you must, but because you are willing, as God wants you to be; not greedy for money, but eager to serve; not lording it over those entrusted to you, but being examples to the flock.

1 PETER 5:2-4

Those who are wise will shine like the brightness of the heavens, and those who lead many to righteousness, like the stars for ever and ever.

DANIEL 12:3

Keep watch over yourselves and all the flock of which the Holy Spirit has made you overseers. Be shepherds of the church of God, which he bought with his own blood.

ACTS 20:28

In your unfailing love you will lead
the people you have redeemed.
In your strength you will guide them
to your holy dwelling.

EXODUS 15:13

If the LORD is pleased with us, he will lead us into that land, a land flowing with milk and honey, and will give it to us.

NUMBERS 14:8

Jesus knew that the Father had put all things under his power, and that he had come from God and was returning to God; so he.... poured water into a basin and began to wash his disciples' feet, drying them with the towel that was wrapped around him.... When Jesus had finished washing their feet, he put on his clothes and returned to his place. "Do you understand what I have done for you?" he asked them. "You call me 'Teacher' and 'Lord,' and rightly so, for that is what I am. Now that I, your Lord and Teacher, have washed your feet, you also should wash one another's feet. I have set you an example that you should do as I have done for you.... now that you know these things, you will be blessed if you do them."

JOHN 13:3–5, 12–15, 17

Don't let anyone look down on you because you are young, but set an example for the believers in speech, in life, in love, in faith and in purity.

1 TIMOTHY 4:12

This is what the LORD says:
"Stand at the crossroads and look;
*   ask for the ancient paths,*
ask where the good way is, and walk in it,
*   and you will find rest for your souls."*

JEREMIAH 6:16

You will receive power when the Holy Spirit comes on you.

ACTS 1:8

REFLECTIONS ON TODAY
for Tomorrow

_____

_____

_____

_____

_____

_____

_____

_____

_____

_____

_____

_____

_____

_____

_____

LONELINESS

My eyes are ever on the LORD,
   for only he will release my feet from the
   snare.
Turn to me , O LORD, and be gracious to me,
   for I am lonely and afflicted.
The troubles of my heart have multiplied;
   free me from my anguish.
Look upon my affliction and my distress
   and take away all my sins. . . .
Guard my life and rescue me;
   let me not be put to shame,
   for I take refuge in you.
May integrity and uprightness protect me,
   because my hope is in you.

PSALM 25:15–18, 20–21

Even though I walk
through the valley of the shadow of death,
I will fear no evil,
for you are with me, O LORD.

PSALM 23:4

I am always with you, LORD,
you hold me by my right hand.

PSALM 73:23

Jesus said, "I will ask the Father, and he will give you another Counselor to be with you forever—the Spirit of truth. The world cannot accept him, because it neither sees him nor knows him. But you know him, for he lives with you and will be in you."

JOHN 14:16–17

Where can I go from your Spirit?
    Where can I flee from your presence?
If I go up to the heavens, you are there;
    if I make my bed in the depths, you are there.
If I rise on the wings of the dawn,
    if I settle on the far side of the sea,
even there your hand will guide me,
    your right hand will hold me fast.
If I say, "Surely the darkness will hide me
    and the light become night around me,"
even the darkness will not be dark to you;
    the night will shine like the day,
    for darkness is as light to you …
I praise you because I am fearfully and
    wonderfully made;
    your works are wonderful, I know that full well.

PSALM 139:7–12, 14

Come near to God and he will come
near to you.

JAMES 4:8

"I am with you and will watch over you wherever you go, and I will bring you back to this land. I will not leave you until I have done what I have promised you," says the LORD.

GENESIS 28:15

This is what the LORD says...
When you pass through the waters,
*   I will be with you;*
and when you pass through the rivers,
*   they will not sweep over you.*
When you walk through the fire,
*   you will not be burned;*
*   the flames will not set you ablaze.*

ISAIAH 43:1—2

God has said,
"Never will I leave you;
*   never will I forsake you."*

HEBREWS 13:5

Jesus said, "I am with you always,
to the very end of the age."

MATTHEW 28:20

In Christ we who are many form one body,
and each member belongs to all the others.

ROMANS 12:5

"If you do whatever I command you
and walk in my ways and do what is right
in my eyes by keeping my statutes and
commands... I will be with you."

1 KINGS 11:38

REFLECTIONS ON TODAY
for Tomorrow

_____

_____

_____

_____

_____

_____

_____

_____

_____

_____

_____

_____

_____

_____

PEACE

Jesus said, "Peace I leave with you; my peace I give you. I do not give to you as the world gives. Do not let your hearts be troubled and do not be afraid."

JOHN 14:27

Great peace have they who love your law, O LORD, and nothing can make them stumble.

PSALM 119:165

"Peace, peace, to those far and near," *says the LORD. "And I will heal them."*

ISAIAH 57:19

God will keep in perfect peace
  him whose mind is steadfast,
  because he trusts in you.

ISAIAH 26:3

Jesus said,
"*Blessed are the peacemakers,*
  for they will be called sons of God."

MATTHEW 5:9

Peacemakers who sow in peace raise a harvest of righteousness.

JAMES 3:18

Jesus himself is our peace.... He came and preached peace to you who were far away and peace to those who were near. For through him we both have access to the Father by one Spirit.

EPHESIANS 2:14, 17–18

The mind controlled by the Spirit is life
and peace.

ROMANS 8:6

I will listen to what God the LORD will say;
he promises peace to his people.

PSALM 85:8

The LORD gives strength to his people;
the LORD blesses his people with peace.

PSALM 29:11

Let the peace of Christ rule in your hearts,
since as members of one body you were
called to peace.

COLOSSIANS 3:15

A heart at peace gives life to the body.

PROVERBS 14:30

Live peaceful and quiet lives in all godliness
and holiness. This is good, and pleases God
our Savior, who wants all men to be saved
and to come to a knowledge of the truth.

1 TIMOTHY 2:2–4

Grace and peace to you from him who is,
and who was, and who is to come.

REVELATION 1:4

Mercy, peace and love be yours in
abundance.

JUDE 1:2

LORD, *you establish peace for us;*
  all that we have accomplished you have
  done for us.

ISAIAH 26:12

May the LORD bless you
and keep you;
May the LORD make his face shine upon you
and be gracious to you;
May the LORD turn his face toward you
and give you peace.

NUMBERS 6:24–26

May the Lord of peace himself give you peace at all times and in every way. The Lord be with all of you.

2 THESSALONIANS 3:16

REFLECTIONS ON TODAY
for Tomorrow

_____

_____

_____

_____

_____

_____

_____

_____

_____

_____

_____

_____

_____

_____

_____

PERSEVERANCE

Consider it pure joy ... whenever you face trials of many kinds, because you know that the testing of your faith develops perseverance. Perseverance must finish its work so that you may be mature and complete, not lacking anything.

JAMES 1:2–4

Blessed is the man who perseveres under trial, because when he has stood the test, he will receive the crown of life that God has promised to those who love him.

JAMES 1:12

Be strong and do not give up, for your work
will be rewarded.

2 CHRONICLES 15:7

Perseverance must finish its work so that
you may be mature and complete, not
lacking anything.

JAMES 1:4–5

Let us not become weary in doing good, for
at the proper time we will reap a harvest if
we do not give up.

GALATIANS 6:9

If we died with Christ,
    we will also live with him;
If we endure,
    we will also reign with him.

2 TIMOTHY 2:11–12

Jesus said, "He who stands firm to the end
will be saved."

MARK 13:13

As you know, we consider blessed those who have persevered. You have heard of Job's perseverance and have seen what the Lord finally brought about. The Lord is full of compassion and mercy.

JAMES 5:11

Do not throw away your confidence; it will be richly rewarded. You need to persevere so that when you have done the will of God, you will receive what he has promised.

HEBREWS 10:35–36

Let us acknowledge the LORD;
     let us press on to acknowledge him.
As surely as the sun rises,
     he will appear;
he will come to us like the winter rains,
     like the spring rains that water the earth.

HOSEA 6:3

My comfort in my suffering is this:
*   Your promise preserves my life.*

PSALM 119:50

My steps have held to your path, O God;
*   my feet have not slipped.*

PSALM 17:5

Stand firm. Let nothing move you. Always give yourselves fully to the work of the Lord, because you know that your labor in the Lord is not in vain.

1 CORINTHIANS 15:58

Since we are surrounded by such a great cloud of witnesses, let us throw off everything that hinders and the sin that so easily entangles, and let us run with perseverance the race marked out for us. Let us fix our eyes on Jesus, the author and perfecter of our faith, who for the joy set before him endured the cross, scorning its shame, and sat down at the right hand of the throne of God. Consider him who endured such opposition from sinful men, so that you will not grow weary and lose heart.

HEBREWS 12:1–3

REFLECTIONS ON TODAY
for Tomorrow

_____

_____

_____

_____

_____

_____

_____

_____

_____

_____

_____

PRAISE

The LORD lives! Praise be to my Rock!
Exalted be God, the Rock, my Savior!

2 SAMUEL 22:47

A voice came from the throne, saying:

"Praise our God,
all you his servants,
you who fear him,
both small and great!"

Then I heard what sounded like a great
multitude, like the roar of rushing waters
and like loud peals of thunder, shouting:

"Hallelujah!
For our Lord God Almighty reigns."

REVELATION 19:5–6

I am like an olive tree
   flourishing in the house of God;
I trust in God's unfailing love
   for ever and ever.
I will praise you forever for what you have done;
   in your name I will hope, for your name
   is good.
   I will praise you in the presence of
   your saints.

PSALM 52:8-9

I will praise you, O LORD, with all my heart;
   I will tell of all your wonders.
I will be glad and rejoice in you;
   I will sing praise to your name,
   O Most High.

PSALM 9:1-2

Fear God and give him glory. ...Worship him who made the heavens, the earth, the sea and the springs of water.

REVELATION 14:7

Come, let us bow down in worship,
let us kneel before the LORD our Maker;
for he is our God
and we are the people of his pasture,
the flock under his care.

PSALM 95:6–7

He is your praise; he is your God.

DEUTERONOMY 10:21

I will praise you, O LORD, among the nations;
I will sing praises to your name.

2 SAMUEL 22:50

Sing praises to God, sing praises;
sing praises to our King, sing praises.
For God is the King of all the earth;
sing to him a psalm of praise.
God reigns over the nations;
God is seated on his holy throne.

PSALM 47:6—8

Praise the LORD, all you nations;
extol him, all you peoples.
For great is his love toward us,
and the faithfulness of the LORD endures
forever.

PSALM 117:1—2

I will sing to the LORD,
*   for he is highly exalted....*
The LORD is my strength and my song;
*   he has become my salvation.*
He is my God, and I will praise him,
*   my father's God, and I will exalt him.*

EXODUS 15:1–2

I will proclaim the name of the Lord.
*   Oh, praise the greatness of our God!*

DEUTERONOMY 32:3

Great is the LORD and most worthy of praise;
*   he is to be feared above all gods.*

1 CHRONICLES 16:25

REFLECTIONS ON TODAY
for Tomorrow

_____

_____

_____

_____

_____

_____

_____

_____

_____

_____

_____

_____

_____

_____

_____

_____

PRAYER

Jesus said, "If you remain in me and my words remain in you, ask whatever you wish, and it will be given you."

JOHN 15:7

Jesus said, "Whatever you ask for in prayer, believe that you have received it, and it will be yours."

MARK 11:24

This is what the LORD says, he who made the earth, the LORD who formed it and established it—the LORD is his name: "Call to me and I will answer you and tell you great and unsearchable things you do not know."

JEREMIAH 33:2–3

Ask the LORD *for rain in the springtime;*
  it is the LORD *who makes the storm clouds.*
He gives showers of rain to men,
  and plants of the field to everyone.

ZECHARIAH 10:1

The righteous cry out, and the LORD *hears them;*
  he delivers them from all their troubles.

PSALM 34:17

I call to God,
  and the LORD *saves me.*
Evening, morning and noon
  I cry out in distress,
  and he hears my voice.

PSALM 55:16–17

Jesus said, "Ask and it will be given to you; seek and you will find; knock and the door will be opened to you. For everyone who asks receives; he who seeks finds; and to him who knocks, the door will be opened."

MATTHEW 7:7–8

"Before [my people] call I will answer;
while they are still speaking I will hear,"
says the LORD.

ISAIAH 65:24

The Spirit helps us in our weakness. We do not know what we ought to pray for, but the Spirit himself intercedes for us with groans that words cannot express.

ROMANS 8:26

This, then, is how you should pray:
"'Our Father in heaven,
hallowed be your name,
your kingdom come,
your will be done
*   on earth as it is in heaven.*
Give us today our daily bread.
Forgive us our debts,
*   as we also have forgiven our debtors.*
And lead us not into temptation,
but deliver us from the evil one.'

MATTHEW 6:9–13

Jesus said, "If two of you on earth agree about anything you ask for, it will be done for you by my Father in heaven."

MATTHEW 18:19

"They will call on my name
  and I will answer them;
I will say, 'They are my people,'
  and they will say, 'The LORD is our God,'"

ZECHARIAH 13:9

In the morning, O LORD, you hear my voice;
  in the morning I lay my requests before you
  and wait in expectation.

PSALM 5:3

How gracious the LORD will be when
you cry for help! As soon as he hears,
he will answer you.

ISAIAH 30:19

REFLECTIONS ON TODAY
for Tomorrow

_____

_____

_____

_____

_____

_____

_____

_____

_____

_____

_____

_____

_____

_____

PRESENCE OF GOD

The LORD said, "My Presence will go with you, and I will give you rest."

EXODUS 33:14

Tremble, O earth, at the presence of the LORD,
*   at the presence of the God of Jacob,*
who turned the rock into a pool,
*   the hard rock into springs of water.*

PSALM 114:7–8

You have made known to me the paths of life;
*   you will fill me with joy in your presence.*

ACTS 2:28

You will call, and the LORD will answer;
you will cry for help, and he will say:
    Here am I.

ISAIAH 58:9

In him we live and move and have our being.

ACTS 17:28

The LORD is with you when you are
with him. If you seek him, he will be
found by you.

2 CHRONICLES 15:2

Jesus said, "Where two or three come
together in my name, there am I with them."

MATTHEW 18:20

Jesus said, "I am the vine; you are the branches. If a man remains in me and I in him, he will bear much fruit."

JOHN 15:5

One thing I ask of the LORD,
*   this is what I seek:*
that I may dwell in the house of the LORD
*   all the days of my life,*
to gaze upon the beauty of the LORD
*   and to seek him in his temple.*

PSALM 27:4

Blessed are those who dwell in your house, O LORD;
*   they are ever praising you.*

PSALM 84:4

I pray that out of his glorious riches he may strengthen you with power through his Spirit in your inner being, so that Christ may dwell in your hearts through faith. And I pray that you, being rooted and established in love, may have power, together with all the saints, to grasp how wide and long and high and deep is the love of Christ, and to know this love that surpasses knowledge— that you may be filled to the measure of all the fullness of God.

EPHESIANS 3:16–19

If the Spirit of him who raised Jesus from the dead is living in you, he who raised Christ from the dead will also give life to your mortal bodies through his Spirit, who lives in you.

ROMANS 8:11

No one has ever seen God; but if we love one another, God lives in us and his love is made complete in us.

1 JOHN 4:12

If ... you seek the LORD your God, you will find him if you look for him with all your heart and with all your soul.

DEUTERONOMY 4:29

God is present in the company of the righteous.

PSALM 14:5

The virgin will be with child and will give birth to a son, and they will call him Immanuel—which means, "God with us."

MATTHEW 1:23

The glory of the LORD fills the whole earth.

NUMBERS 14:21

REFLECTIONS ON TODAY
for Tomorrow

_____

_____

_____

_____

_____

_____

_____

_____

_____

_____

_____

_____

_____

_____

PROTECTION

I lift up my eyes to the hills—
*   where does my help come from?*
*My help comes from the L*ORD*,*
*   the Maker of heaven and earth.*
He will not let your foot slip—
*   he who watches over you will not slumber; . . .*
*The L*ORD *watches over you—*
*   the L*ORD *is your shade at your right hand;*
the sun will not harm you by day,
*   nor the moon by night.*
*The L*ORD *will keep you from all harm—*
*   he will watch over your life;*
*the L*ORD *will watch over your coming and going*
*   both now and forevermore.*

PSALM 121:1–3, 5–8

Jesus said, "Everyone who hears these words of mine and puts them into practice is like a wise man who built his house on the rock. The rain came down, the streams rose, and the winds blew and beat against that house; yet it did not fall, because it had its foundation on the rock."

MATTHEW 7:24–25

Jesus prayed, "I pray for [my disciples]. I am not praying for the world, but for those you have given me, for they are yours. All I have is yours, and all you have is mine. And glory has come to me through them. I will remain in the world no longer, but they are still in the world, and I am coming to you. Holy Father, protect them by the power of your name—the name you gave me—so that they may be one as we are one.

JOHN 17:9–11

O my Strength, I watch for you;
*   you, O God, are my fortress, my loving God.*

PSALM 59:9–10

Blessed is he who has regard for the weak;
*   the LORD delivers him in times of trouble.*
The LORD will protect him and preserve his life;
*   he will bless him in the land.*

PSALM 41:1–2

The LORD guards the course of the just
*   and protects the way of his faithful ones.*
Then you will understand what is right and just
*   and fair—every good path.*

PROVERBS 2:8–9

You are my hiding place, LORD;
*   you will protect me from trouble*
and surround me with songs of deliverance.

PSALM 32:7

The LORD will cover you with his feathers,
and under his wings you will find refuge;
his faithfulness will be your shield and
rampart.
You will not fear the terror of night,
nor the arrow that flies by day.

PSALM 91:4–5

If you make the Most High your dwelling—
even the LORD, who is my refuge—
then no harm will befall you,
no disaster will come near your tent.
For he will command his angels concerning you
to guard you in all your ways.

PSALM 91:9–11

"Because he loves me," says the LORD,
     "I will rescue him;
     I will protect him, for he acknowledges
     my name.
He will call upon me, and I will answer him;
     I will be with him in trouble,
     I will deliver him and honor him.
With long life will I satisfy him
     and show him my salvation."

PSALM 91:14–16

The name of the LORD is a strong tower;
     the righteous run to it and are safe.

PROVERBS 18:10

The way of the LORD is a refuge for the righteous.

PROVERBS 10:29

REFLECTIONS ON TODAY
for Tomorrow

_____

_____

_____

_____

_____

_____

_____

_____

_____

_____

_____

_____

RELATIONSHIPS

I am a friend to all who fear you,
to all who follow your precepts.
The earth is filled with your love, O LORD;
teach me your decrees.

PSALM 119:63–64

He who loves a pure heart and whose speech
is gracious
will have the king for his friend.

PROVERBS 22:11

Bear with each other and forgive whatever
grievances you may have against one
another. Forgive as the Lord forgave you.

COLOSSIANS 3:13

Perfume and incense bring joy to the heart,
    and the pleasantness of one's friend springs
    from his earnest counsel.

PROVERBS 27:9

"Do not seek revenge or bear a grudge against one of your people, but love your neighbor as yourself. I am the LORD."

LEVITICUS 19:18

"No longer will a man teach his neighbor,
    or a man his brother, saying,
    'Know the LORD,'
because they will all know me,
    from the least of them to the greatest,"
        declares the LORD.

JEREMIAH 31:34

A friend loves at all times.

PROVERBS 17:17

Two are better than one,
*   because they have a good return for*
*   their work.*
If one falls down,
*   his friend can help him up.*

ECCLESIASTES 4:9–10

He who walks with the wise grows wise.

PROVERBS 13:20

Be devoted to one another in brotherly love.
Honor one another above yourselves.

ROMANS 12:10

If we walk in the light, as he is in the light,
we have fellowship with one another.

1 JOHN 1:7

Let no debt remain outstanding, except
the continuing debt to love one another,
for he who loves his fellowman has fulfilled
the law.

ROMANS 13:8

Jesus said, "I tell you the truth, whatever
you did for one of the least of these brothers
of mine, you did for me."

MATTHEW 25:40

[The new believers] who accepted his message were baptized. . . . They devoted themselves to the apostles' teaching and to the fellowship, to the breaking of bread and to prayer. Everyone was filled with awe, and many wonders and miraculous signs were done by the apostles. All the believers were together and had everything in common. Selling their possessions and goods, they gave to anyone as he had need. Every day they continued to meet together in the temple courts. They broke bread in their homes and ate together with glad and sincere hearts, praising God and enjoying the favor of all the people. And the Lord added to their number daily those who were being saved.

ACTS 2:41–47

REFLECTIONS ON TODAY
for Tomorrow

_____

_____

_____

_____

_____

_____

_____

_____

_____

_____

_____

_____

_____

RIGHTEOUSNESS

Jesus said,
"Blessed are those who hunger and thirst for
    righteousness,
        for they will be filled.
Blessed are those who are persecuted because
    of righteousness,
        for theirs is the kingdom of heaven.

MATTHEW 5:6, 10

He who pursues righteousness and love
    finds life, prosperity and honor.

PROVERBS 21:21

Sow for yourselves righteousness,
*   reap the fruit of unfailing love,*
and break up your unplowed ground;
*   for it is time to seek the* LORD,
until he comes
*   and showers righteousness on you.*

HOSEA 10:12

Now a righteousness from God, apart from law, has been made known, to which the Law and the Prophets testify. This righteousness from God comes through faith in Jesus Christ to all who believe.

ROMANS 3:21—22

Good will come to him who is generous
*   and lends freely,*
*   who conducts his affairs with justice.*
Surely he will never be shaken;
*   a righteous man will be remembered forever.*

PSALM 112:5—6

The mouth of the righteous man utters wisdom,
and his tongue speaks what is just.
The law of his God is in his heart;
his feet do not slip.

Psalm 37:30–31

If you know that [Jesus] is righteous, you
know that everyone who does what is right
has been born of him.

1 John 2:29

God does not take his eyes off the righteous;
he enthrones them with kings
and exalts them forever.

Job 36:7

The LORD is righteous in all his ways
and loving toward all he has made.

Righteous are you, O LORD,
and your laws are right.
The statutes you have laid down are righteous;
they are fully trustworthy.

PSALM 119:137–138

God made him who had no sin to be sin for us, so that in him we might become the righteousness of God.

2 CORINTHIANS 5:21

He himself bore our sins in his body on the tree, so that we might die to sins and live for righteousness; by his wounds you have been healed.

1 PETER 2:24

It is because of him that you are in Christ
Jesus, who has become for us wisdom from
God—that is, our righteousness, holiness
and redemption.

1 CORINTHIANS 1:30

The fruit of righteousness will be peace;
    the effect of righteousness will be quietness
    and confidence forever.

ISAIAH 32:17

REFLECTIONS ON TODAY
for Tomorrow

_____

_____

_____

_____

_____

_____

_____

_____

_____

_____

_____

_____

_____

_____

SECURITY

I am convinced that neither death nor life,
neither angels nor demons, neither the
present nor the future, nor any powers,
neither height nor depth, nor anything else
in all creation, will be able to separate us
from the love of God that is in Christ Jesus
our Lord.

ROMANS 8:38–39

The LORD said, "I will heal my people
and will let them enjoy abundant peace
and security."

JEREMIAH 33:6

He who walks in wisdom is kept safe.

PROVERBS 28:26

The angel of the Lord encamps around those who
> *fear him,*
>> *and he delivers them.*

PSALM 34:7

The Lord himself goes before you and
will be with you; he will never leave you
nor forsake you. Do not be afraid;
do not be discouraged.

DEUTERONOMY 31:8

> *May those who love the Lord be secure.*
> *May there be peace within your walls*
>> *and security within your citadels.*

PSALM 122:6

"Follow my decrees and be careful to obey
my laws, and you will live safely in the land.
Then the land will yield its fruit, and you
will eat your fill and live there in safety,"
says the Lord.

LEVITICUS 25:18–19

I have set the LORD always before me.
Because he is at my right hand,
I will not be shaken.
Therefore my heart is glad and my tongue rejoices;
my body also will rest secure.

PSALM 16:8–9

O righteous God,
who searches minds and hearts ...
make the righteous secure.

PSALM 7:9

You will be secure, because there is hope;
you will look about you and take your
rest in safety.

JOB 11:18

Blessed is the man who trusts in the LORD,
  whose confidence is in him.
He will be like a tree planted by the water
  that sends out its roots by the stream.
It does not fear when heat comes;
  its leaves are always green.
It has no worries in a year of drought
  and never fails to bear fruit.

JEREMIAH 17:7–8

Jesus said, "Are not two sparrows sold for a penny? Yet not one of them will fall to the ground apart from the will of your Father. And even the very hairs of your head are all numbered. So don't be afraid; you are worth more than many sparrows."

MATTHEW 10:29–31

Keep me safe, O God,
for in you I take refuge....
LORD, you have assigned me my portion
and my cup;
You have made my lot secure.

PSALM 16:1, 5

Love and faithfulness keep a king safe;
through love his throne is made secure.

PROVERBS 20:28

REFLECTIONS ON TODAY
for Tomorrow

SERVING

Acknowledge the God of your father, and serve him with wholehearted devotion and with a willing mind, for the LORD searches every heart and understands every motive behind the thoughts.

1 CHRONICLES 28:9

The Lord redeems his servants;
*   no one will be condemned who takes*
*   refuge in him.*

PSALM 34:22

The LORD has chosen you to stand before him and serve him.

2 CHRONICLES 29:11

Whatever you do, work at it with all your heart, as working for the Lord, not for men, since you know that you will receive an inheritance from the Lord as a reward. It is the Lord Christ you are serving.

COLOSSIANS 3:23–24

Keep your spiritual fervor, serving the Lord.

ROMANS 12:11

Jesus said, "Whoever wants to become great among you must be your servant, and whoever wants to be first must be slave of all. For even the Son of Man did not come to be served, but to serve, and to give his life as a ransom for many."

MARK 10:43–45

If anyone speaks, he should do it as one speaking the very words of God. If anyone serves, he should do it with the strength God provides, so that in all things God may be praised through Jesus Christ. To him be the glory and the power for ever and ever. Amen.

1 PETER 4:11

Serve wholeheartedly, as if you were serving the Lord, not men, because you know that the Lord will reward everyone for whatever good he does.

EPHESIANS 6:7–8

Jesus said, "The greatest among you should be like the youngest, and the one who rules like the one who serves. For who is greater, the one who is at the table or the one who serves? Is it not the one who is at the table? But I am among you as one who serves."

LUKE 22:26–27

Jesus said, "It is written: Worship the Lord your God and serve him only."

LUKE 4:8

If [a man's gift] is serving, let him serve; if it is teaching, let him teach; if it is encouraging, let him encourage; if it is contributing to the needs of others, let him give generously; if it is leadership, let him govern diligently; if it is showing mercy, let him do it cheerfully.

ROMANS 12:7–8

Jesus said, "Whoever serves me must follow me; and where I am, my servant also will be. My Father will honor the one who serves me."

JOHN 12:26

Jesus said, "I have set you an example that you should do as I have done for you. I tell you the truth, no servant is greater than his master, nor is a messenger greater than the one who sent him. Now that you know these things, you will be blessed if you do them."

JOHN 13:15–17

It is the LORD your God you must follow, and him you must revere. Keep his commands and obey him; serve him and hold fast to him.

DEUTERONOMY 13:4

May the favor of the LORD our God rest upon us; establish the work of our hands for us— yes, establish the work of our hands.

PSALM 90:17

REFLECTIONS ON TODAY
for Tomorrow

STRENGTH

"Do not fear, for I am with you;
do not be dismayed, for I am your God.
I will strengthen you and help you;
I will uphold you with my righteous
right hand."

ISAIAH 41:10

My flesh and my heart may fail,
but God is the strength of my heart
and my portion forever.

PSALM 73:26

May he strengthen your hearts so that you
will be blameless and holy in the presence of
our God and Father when our Lord Jesus
comes with all his holy ones.

1 THESSALONIANS 3:13

Surely God is my salvation;
 I will trust and not be afraid.
The Lord, the Lord, is my strength
 and my song;
 he has become my salvation.

ISAIAH 12:2

The Lord said, "My grace is sufficient for you, for my power is made perfect in weakness." Therefore I will boast all the more gladly about my weaknesses, so that Christ's power may rest on me. That is why, for Christ's sake, I delight in weaknesses, in insults, in hardships, in persecutions, in difficulties. For when I am weak, then I am strong.

2 CORINTHIANS 12:9–10

"I will search for the lost and bring back the strays. I will bind up the injured and strengthen the weak … I will shepherd the flock with justice," declares the Sovereign Lord.

EZEKIEL 34:16

I will sing of your strength,
  in the morning I will sing of your love;
for you are my fortress,
  my refuge in times of trouble.
O my Strength, I sing praise to you;
  you, O God, are my fortress, my loving God.

PSALM 59:16–17

God is our refuge and strength,
  an ever-present help in trouble.

PSALM 46:1

The LORD gives strength to his people;
  the LORD blesses his people with peace.

PSALM 29:11

The LORD is the strength of his people,
  a fortress of salvation for his anointed one.

PSALM 28:8

He will keep you strong to the end, so that you will be blameless on the day of our Lord Jesus Christ.

1 CORINTHIANS 1:8

In repentance and rest is your salvation,
in quietness and trust is your strength.

ISAIAH 30:15

The righteous will hold to their ways,
and those with clean hands will
grow stronger.

JOB 17:9

This is what the LORD *says:*
"*Let not the wise man boast of his wisdom*
  or the strong man boast of his strength
  or the rich man boast of his riches,
but let him who boasts boast about this:
  that he understands and knows me,
that I am the LORD, *who exercises kindness,*
  justice and righteousness on earth,
  for in these I delight.

JEREMIAH 9 : 2 3 — 2 4

The Lord stood at my side and gave
me strength.

2 TIMOTHY 4 : 1 7

REFLECTIONS ON TODAY
for Tomorrow

_____

_____

_____

_____

_____

_____

_____

_____

_____

_____

_____

_____

STRESS

Praise be to the LORD, to God our Savior,
  who daily bears our burdens.

PSALM 68:19

Submit to God and be at peace with him;
  in this way prosperity will come to you....
You will pray to him, and he will hear you,
  and you will fulfill your vows.
What you decide on will be done,
  and light will shine on your ways.

JOB 22:21, 27–28

"I will refresh the weary and satisfy the
faint," says the LORD.

JEREMIAH 31:25

When God gives any man wealth and possessions, and enables him to enjoy them, to accept his lot and be happy in his work—this is a gift of God. He seldom reflects on the days of his life, because God keeps him occupied with gladness of heart.

ECCLESIASTES 5:19–20

Because so many people were coming and going that they did not even have a chance to eat, Jesus said to them, "Come with me by yourselves to a quiet place and get some rest."

MARK 6:31

God has made me forget all my trouble.

GENESIS 41:51

The LORD is a refuge for the oppressed,
    a stronghold in times of trouble.

PSALM 9:9

Answer me when I call to you,
    O my righteous God.
Give me relief from my distress;
    be merciful to me and hear my prayer.

PSALM 4:1

In all their distress he too was distressed,
    and the angel of his presence saved them.
In his love and mercy he redeemed them;
    he lifted them up and carried them
    all the days of old.

ISAIAH 63:9

Jesus said, "Come to me, all you who are weary and burdened, and I will give you rest. Take my yoke upon you and learn from me, for I am gentle and humble in heart, and you will find rest for your souls. For my yoke is easy and my burden is light."

MATTHEW 11:28–30

In the day of my trouble I will call to you,
* for you will answer me, O LORD.*

PSALM 86:7

God said, "In your distress you called and I
* rescued you."*

PSALM 81:7

Jesus said, "With God all things are possible."

MATTHEW 19:26

By the seventh day God had finished the work he had been doing; so on the seventh day he rested from all his work. And God blessed the seventh day and made it holy, because on it he rested from all the work of creating that he had done.

GENESIS 2:2–3

There remains, then, a Sabbath-rest for the people of God; for anyone who enters God's rest also rests from his own work, just as God did from his. Let us, therefore, make every effort to enter that rest.

HEBREWS 4:9–11

Great peace have they who love your law, O LORD, and nothing can make them stumble.

PSALM 119:165

REFLECTIONS ON TODAY
for Tomorrow

_____

_____

_____

_____

_____

_____

_____

_____

_____

_____

_____

_____

TRUST

Let the morning bring me word of your
    unfailing love,
        for I have put my trust in you.
Show me the way I should go,
        for to you I lift up my soul.

PSALM 143:8

Commit your way to the LORD;
        trust in him and he will do this:
He will make your righteousness shine like
    the dawn,
        the justice of your cause like the noonday sun.

PSALM 37:5—6

*Those who trust in the L*ORD *are like Mount Zion,*
which cannot be shaken but endures forever.

PSALM 125:1

I am still confident of this:
*I will see the goodness of the L*ORD
in the land of the living.
*Wait for the L*ORD*;*
be strong and take heart
and wait for the Lord.

PSALM 27:13–14

*The L*ORD*'s unfailing love*
surrounds the man who trusts in him.

PSALM 32:10

Anyone who trusts in the Lord will never be
put to shame.

ROMANS 10:11

I know that the LORD saves his anointed;
he answers him from his holy heaven
with the saving power of his right hand.
Some trust in chariots and some in horses,
but we trust in the name of the LORD our God.
They are brought to their knees and fall,
but we rise up and stand firm.

PSALM 20:6–8

This is what the Sovereign LORD says:
"See, I lay a stone in Zion,
a tested stone,
a precious cornerstone for a sure foundation;
the one who trusts will never be dismayed.

ISAIAH 28:16

You are enthroned as the Holy One;
    you are the praise of Israel.
In you our fathers put their trust;
    they trusted and you delivered them.
They cried to you and were saved;
    in you they trusted and were not
    disappointed.

PSALM 22:3–5

O Sovereign LORD, you are God! Your
words are trustworthy.

2 SAMUEL 7:28

I trust in God's unfailing love
    for ever and ever.

PSALM 52:8

Guard my life, for I am devoted to you.
    You are my God; save your servant
    who trusts in you.

PSALM 86:2

The law of the LORD is perfect,
    reviving the soul.
The statutes of the LORD are trustworthy,
    making wise the simple.

PSALM 19:7

Surely this is our God;
    we trusted in him, and he saved us.
This is the LORD, we trusted in him;
    let us rejoice and be glad in
    his salvation.

ISAIAH 25:9

REFLECTIONS ON TODAY
for Tomorrow

_____

_____

_____

_____

_____

_____

_____

_____

_____

_____

_____

_____

_____

WILL OF GOD

In Christ we were also chosen, having been predestined according to the plan of him who works out everything in conformity with the purpose of his will, in order that we, who were the first to hope in Christ, might be for the praise of his glory.

EPHESIANS 1:11–12

May the God of peace … equip you with everything good for doing his will, and may he work in us what is pleasing to him, through Jesus Christ, to whom be glory for ever and ever. Amen.

HEBREWS 13:20–21

Be transformed by the renewing of your mind. Then you will be able to test and approve what God's will is—his good, pleasing and perfect will.

ROMANS 12:2

Grace and peace to you from God our Father and the Lord Jesus Christ, who gave himself for our sins to rescue us from the present evil age, according to the will of our God and Father, to whom be glory for ever and ever. Amen.

GALATIANS 1:3–5

Jesus declared, "I have come down from heaven not to do my will but to do the will of him who sent me. And this is the will of him who sent me, that I shall lose none of all that he has given me, but raise them up at the last day."

JOHN 6:38-39

You ought to say, "If it is the Lord's will, we will live and do this or that."

JAMES 4:15

Be joyful always; pray continually; give thanks in all circumstances, for this is God's will for you in Christ Jesus.

1 THESSALONIANS 5:16–18

Jesus said, "If anyone chooses to do God's will, he will find out whether my teaching comes from God or whether I speak on my own. He who speaks on his own does so to gain honor for himself, but he who works for the honor of the one who sent him is a man of truth; there is nothing false about him."

JOHN 7:17–18

The world and its desires pass away, but the man who does the will of God lives forever.

1 JOHN 2:17

He who searches our hearts knows the mind of the Spirit, because the Spirit intercedes for the saints in accordance with God's will.

ROMANS 8:27

Jesus said, "Whoever does the will of my Father in heaven is my brother and sister and mother."

MATTHEW 12:50

Teach me to do your will,
for you are my God;
may your good Spirit
lead me on level ground.

PSALM 143:10

It is God's will that you should be
sanctified ... that each of you should learn
to control his own body in a way that is
holy and honorable.

1 THESSALONIANS 4:3-4

Those who suffer according to God's will
should commit themselves to their faithful
Creator and continue to do good.

1 PETER 4:19

Stand firm in all the will of God, mature
and fully assured.

COLOSSIANS 4:12

REFLECTIONS ON TODAY
for Tomorrow

_____

_____

_____

_____

_____

_____

_____

_____

_____

_____

_____

_____

_____

_____

WISDOM

The fear of the LORD is the beginning of wisdom;
all who follow his precepts have good
understanding.
To him belongs eternal praise.

PSALM 111:10

The foolishness of God is wiser than man's
wisdom, and the weakness of God is
stronger than man's strength.

1 CORINTHIANS 1:25

Wisdom is supreme; therefore get wisdom.
Though it cost all you have, get
understanding.

PROVERBS 4:7

Praise and glory
and wisdom and thanks and honor
and power and strength
be to our God for ever and ever.
    Amen!

REVELATION 7:12

How much better to get wisdom than gold,
    to choose understanding rather than silver!

PROVERBS 16:16

Wisdom, like an inheritance, is a good thing
    and benefits those who see the sun.
Wisdom is a shelter
    as money is a shelter,
but the advantage of knowledge is this:
    that wisdom preserves the life of its possessor.

ECCLESIASTES 7:11–12

Wisdom makes one wise man more powerful
than ten rulers in a city.

ECCLESIASTES 7:19

The wisdom that comes from heaven is first of all pure; then peace-loving, considerate, submissive, full of mercy and good fruit, impartial and sincere.

JAMES 3:17

Who is like the wise man?
Who knows the explanation of things?
Wisdom brightens a man's face
and changes its hard appearance.

ECCLESIASTES 8:1

By wisdom a house is built,
and through understanding it
is established;
through knowledge its rooms are filled
with rare and beautiful treasures.

PROVERBS 24:3–4

Blessed is the man who finds wisdom,
the man who gains understanding,
for she is more profitable than silver
and yields better returns than gold.

PROVERBS 3:13–14

He who gets wisdom loves his own soul;
he who cherishes understanding prospers.

PROVERBS 19:8

If you accept my words
and store up my commands within you,
turning your ear to wisdom
and applying your heart to understanding,
and if you call out for insight
and cry aloud for understanding,
and if you look for it as for silver
and search for it as for hidden treasure,
then you will understand the fear of the LORD
and find the knowledge of God.

PROVERBS 2:1–5

A man's wisdom gives him patience;
it is to his glory to overlook an offense.

PROVERBS 19:11

REFLECTIONS ON TODAY
for Tomorrow

_____

_____

_____

_____

_____

_____

_____

_____

_____

_____

_____

_____

WORRY

Do not be anxious about anything, but in everything, by prayer and petition, with thanksgiving, present your requests to God. And the peace of God, which transcends all understanding, will guard your hearts and your minds in Christ Jesus.

PHILIPPIANS 4:6–7

Search me, O God, and know my heart;
test me and know my anxious thoughts.

PSALM 139:23

Banish anxiety from your heart
and cast off the troubles of your body.

ECCLESIASTES 11:10

Our light and momentary troubles are achieving for us an eternal glory that far outweighs them all.

2 CORINTHIANS 4:17

"I am the LORD, the God of all mankind. Is anything too hard for me?"

JEREMIAH 32:27

God is able to do immeasurably more than all we ask or imagine.

EPHESIANS 3:20

Jesus said, "Do not let your hearts be troubled. Trust in God; trust also in me."

JOHN 14:1

Jesus said, "Who of you by worrying can add a single hour to his life? Since you cannot do this very little thing, why do you worry about the rest?

"Consider how the lilies grow. They do not labor or spin. Yet I tell you, not even Solomon in all his splendor was dressed like one of these. If that is how God clothes the grass of the field, which is here today, and tomorrow is thrown into the fire, how much more will he clothe you, O you of little faith! And do not set your heart on what you will eat or drink; do not worry about it. For the pagan world runs after all such things, and your Father knows that you need them. But seek his kingdom, and these things will be given to you as well."

LUKE 12:25–31

The LORD watches over you—
*   the LORD is your shade at your right hand;*
the sun will not harm you by day,
*   nor the moon by night.*
The LORD will keep you from all harm—
*   he will watch over your life;*
the LORD will watch over your coming and going
*   both now and forevermore.*

PSALM 121:5–8

"No one will be able to stand up against you all the days of your life. As I was with Moses, so I will be with you; I will never leave you nor forsake you," says the LORD.

JOSHUA 1:5

Promises and Prayers for You in the Military
Copyright © 2003 by The Zondervan Corporation
ISBN 0-310-80576-7

Requests for information should be addressed to:
Inspirio, The gift group of Zondervan
Grand Rapids, Michigan 49530
http://www.inspiriogifts.com

Compiler: Merry E. Marter
Editor: Janice Jacobson
Design Manager: Amy J. Wenger
Design: UDG|DesignWorks, Sisters Oregon

Printed in USA
02 03 04/DP/ 4 3 2 1

To

_____

From

....

Jesus said, "Peace I leave with you;
my peace I give you. I do not give to you as
the world gives. Do not let your hearts be
troubled and do not be afraid.

JOHN 14:27